Working and Thinking on the Waterfront

Books by Eric Hoffer

The True Believer

The Passionate State of Mind

The Ordeal of Change

The Temper of Our Time

Working and Thinking on the Waterfront

First Things, Last Things

Reflections on the Human Condition

In Our Time

Before the Sabbath

Between the Devil and the Dragon

Truth Imagined

Working and Thinking on the Waterfront

Eric Hoffer

Hopewell Publications

Published by Hopewell
Publications, LLC
PO Box 11, Titusville, NJ
08560-0011 (609) 818-1049

info@HopePubs.com
www.HopePubs.com

International Standard Book Number: 9781933435299

Library of Congress Control Number: 2009931969

First Edition

Printed in the United States of America

Graphics derived from the Hoffer estate private archives

I prefer the company of peasants because they have not been educated sufficiently to reason incorrectly.

- Michel de Montaigne

Preface

While rummaging recently through a pile of old notebooks, I came upon a diary I had kept during 1958-1959. I had completely forgotten about it. Nineteen fifty-eight and 1959 were difficult years. I was trying to write a book on the intellectuals, the "men of words." Since it was not going to be a scholarly history, it soon became clear that my theories and insights would not come to more than fifty pages of manuscript—enough for a chapter but not a book. Obviously, the intellectual would have to be part of a larger subject. I began to suspect that all my thinking life I had probably had only one train of thought, that everything I had written stemmed from a central preoccupation, and that I might go through life and never discover what it was.

I had to sort things out; talk to somebody. So on June 1, 1958, I began a diary. Toward the end of March, 1959, I realized that my central subject was change. I knew I would have to write two small books: one on change in the backward countries and one on change in general.

The diary filled seven notebooks. The entry on the last pages of the seventh notebook was for May 21, 1959. I cannot remember what decided me not to go on with the diary. I did not start another notebook.

It is perhaps not out of place to state here plainly what I mean by intellectuals. They are people who feel themselves members of the educated minority, with a God-given right to direct and shape events. An intellectual need not be well educated or particularly intelligent. What counts is the feeling of being a member of an educated elite.

An intellectual wants to be listened to. He wants to instruct and to be taken seriously. It is more important to him to be important than to be free, and he would rather be persecuted than ignored. Typical intellectuals feel oppressed in a democratic society where they are left alone, to do as they please. They call it jester's license, and they envy intellectuals in Communist countries who are persecuted by governments that take intellectuals seriously.

E.H.

Working and Thinking on the Waterfront

June 1, 1958

5 A.M. I am getting self-righteous. This usually happens after a long stretch of work. I remember Tolstoi saying somewhere that work makes not only ants but men, too, cruel.

4 P.M. Went to the dentist to have my teeth cleaned. Lili and the boy met me afterwards and we went to the beach. We had a good, plentiful meal at the Hitchrack. It is long since I tasted such good liver. The boy has learned several dirty words. Lili does not seem alarmed.

10 P.M. Went to the union meeting. Again the contrast between the shallowness of the discussion of the abstract and the originality in tackling the practical. There were weariness and boredom in the first half of the meeting, which dealt with the Sobell* case. In the second half the subject was the hiring hall and how to deal with chiselers on the scrap-iron jobs. The solutions offered were original and wonderfully simple. The simplicity gave an impression of subtlety.

It would be fascinating to see whether the longshoremen's originality in solving practical problems could be canalized into theorizing and the play with ideas. We know of a canalization in the opposite direction. In the middle of the nineteenth century the

---

* Morton Sobell was convicted as a spy in 1951, in connection with the Rosenberg case. The radicals are still agitating for his release.

intellectual energy of New England was drained into the practical channels of mining, engineering, railroading, and the like, during the opening of the West. The feats of practical organization of the Rockefellers, Morgans, and even the Carnegies were the feats of potential philosophers plunged into an atmosphere of action.

I am aware of how much I have to watch myself. The pitfalls are all around me: not only self-righteousness but also a deprecation of others. The others are not the people I work and live with but the intellectuals in general. There is a danger I might come to think of most of them as sterile, pretentious, and futile. And it is strange that this attitude should become pronounced at a time when my creative flow is at its thinnest.

June 2

The present depression, even if it turns out to be temporary, and our lag in science and technology have shaken my confidence. The disillusionment with America is not likely to follow the course of the disillusionment with Britain which we experienced between the two world wars. The chief weakness in this country is the inability to keep the industrial plant in full operation all the time. The weakness in England was that it had to sustain an edifice of Empire on a shaky economic foundation. I doubt whether being or not being a great world power would deeply affect our lives in this country. What matters is the crisis of confidence in our know-how and ingenuity.

I am cheered when I realize that things vital for my welfare or prospects have completely escaped my mind. Preoccupation with the self has always seemed to me unhealthy.

The analysts and prognosticators have not shown up well on the French crisis. In this case the man in the street was a better judge than the experts. To an intellectual, words—parliament, democracy, dictatorship, fascism—loom large. To the general run of people the chief question is whether, and how smoothly, a thing works. The government of France, call it by any name, has not worked during the past decades. To make it work you have to get it out of the hands of the people who have played with it until now.

June 4

Nine hours on the German ship *Dortheim* at Pier 26.

On the way to the job it occurred to me that the homogenizing effect of Communism is partly due to its inducement of passionate rudeness. People of all nationalities become somewhat alike when swept away by a fit of rudeness.

On the job I had for a partner the voluble Negro, "Cigar" Barlow. He is a fairly effective speaker at union meeting, somewhat of a rabble-rouser, but his conversation is pretentious and empty. He had gone to see and hear Billy Graham, but could not tell me why he was so impressed. He uses high-sounding clichés.

Character seems to be more typical among Negroes than among Whites. The unctuous hypocrite, the barefaced cheat, the windbag, the lecher, the miser are immediately identifiable, and remind one of types one has read about in old books and fairytales. There must be a large element of playacting in the Negro's life. My hunch is that any change in the fortunes of a Negro would immediately show itself in every detail of his life. There will be a new play, and a new role acted with minute attention to every detail.

On and off during the day I have been thinking about woman's role in American political life. My feeling is that, on the whole, women will vote against the workingman. They will side with anything that smacks of an upper or ruling class. Women elected Eisenhower, and they were shocked by Truman's commonness.

June 5

Finished the German ship at Pier 26. Six hours. I have the impression that many Scandinavian longshoremen are anti-British. They speak of the British the way the anti-Semites speak of the Jews. According to Axel (the Swede I talked with today) the British own every mine, mill, and factory in Sweden, Norway, and Denmark. How come then that Britain seems to be hard up? Answer: it's only the poor in Britain who are hard up.

It is perhaps true that ignorance tends to be extremist. Our opinions about things we do not know are not likely to be balanced and moderate.

My mind went back to the possibility of canalizing practical intelligence into intellectual channels. One of the peculiarities of the Occident has been the ability to distill spiritual impulses from practical pursuits. The Italian Renaissance was born in the market-place, in the workshops of artisans. Pure science emerged from the pursuits of architects, navigators, and craftsmen. The Greeks extracted geometry from surveying, and their philosophy probably received its first impetus from the invention of coinage about 700 B.C. It was but a step from seeing coins as the common denominator of all values to the speculations that the manifold appearance of things is due to different states and arrangements of a fundamental substance.

June 6

Four hours on the *Lurline* at Pier 35. In the afternoon I took Lili and the boy to the circus. The child seemed hardly interested in the stunts and spectacles. My impression is that he can get excited only about something that has a direct relationship to him. In the zoo and in the park there is a personal confrontation between the animals and himself. This lack of enthusiasm for the circus reminded me that he shows no interest in animated toys such as pecking birds and other mechanical animals. He becomes passionately attached to the sculpture of a bird or an animal, no matter how crude, and he spends hours tinkering with wheels and gears.

June 8

A long day, loading rice on the *Hawaiian Pilot* in Encinal. There have been intermittent downpours. Had it not been for the pleasantness of my partner it would have been a miserable day. Between loads I observed sparrows feeding on patches of scattered rice on the dock. How timid they are! Are there blobs of life without fear? They come down from the edge of the roof like a cloud, and spread out like a carpet. They seem to keep away from spots where the rice is thick as if fearing a snare.

June 10

Didn't do a thing! Took Lili and the child to lunch and then to the Indian exhibition at the Palace of the Legion of Honor.

I was roused by an article in the latest *Nation*. It was written by a fellow named Halevy who is obviously an American writer living in Mexico. He has recently paid a visit to the U.S., and his article deals with Disneyland and Las Vegas. My impression is as follows: The man is some sort of a radical, and is extremely money-conscious. He is contemptuous of people who throwaway their money. Chances are he made some money in real estate and went to Mexico, where living is cheap, to write. His contempt for America is standard. In one sentence he says we worship the almighty buck, and in the next he grinds his teeth at the levity and stupidity with which we throw away our money. He resolves the paradox by saying that our wasting is a way of punishing our idols.

The article tells little about this country but a lot about the writer. I am often struck by the money-consciousness of many radicals and their skill in business, particularly in real estate. The radicals on the waterfront have left-wing principles and right-wing bank accounts.

June 11

Eight hours on the sorting pile at Pier 29. As hard a day as I have had in a long time. This company has finally figured out how to keep people going without a pause. No sooner is one row of loads started than another row is all lined up waiting for you. I run up a sweat all day long partly because of the heat and partly because of the rushing.

The *Manchester Guardian Weekly* is suggesting that De Gaulle, if not a fool, is a weak sister. Some letter writer sees De Gaulle as a Hindenburg who unknowingly prepares the ground for a Hitler. My feeling is that whatever authoritarian regime may arise in France it will be tempered by rationality and good sense.

June 12

The whole morning I fought the impulse to meet Little Eric as he comes out of the nursery school. My attachment to the boy is being reinforced by a sense of loneliness. Men feel lonely when they do not do the one thing they ought to do. It is only when we fully exercise our capacities—when we grow—that we have roots in the world and feel at home in it.

I have been reading a couple of articles on Russian science (one in the *Nation* and the other in *Commentary*). They confirmed my suspicion that freedom is not indispensable for cultural creativeness. A despotism that respects and subsidizes science, literature, and art can be a good milieu for creativeness in these fields.

9 P.M. Have just returned from seeing a French picture—a crime story, *The Girl on the Third Floor*. It is a civilized picture.

The criminals seem humane, and everyone is rational. Not too exciting, but it kept me fully interested for 1½ hours.

June 13

Seven hours on the Norwegian ship *Hoegh Silverstream*. Rubber wrapped in burlap or paper. Partner one of the laziest men on the waterfront, yet he worked well and was pleasant. He is, however, a total, pathological liar, hence conversation with him is meaningless. For a moment it seemed to me that only conversation about ideas can be honest. Most other talk is nine-tenths make-believe.

At noon I heard a Sicilian proverb: "The tongue has no bones, but it can break bones."

In the afternoon a young clerk came over to talk with me. He is a graduate of the University of San Francisco, fairly intelligent, pious, and superficial. I talked a lot and it did me good. Yesterday I spent twenty-four hours without talking to anyone, so I needed talking.

June 14

Pier 26. British ship. Discharging meat and apples from New Zealand. The apples, Rome Beauties, are as fine as any I have seen.

The British crew on this ship makes an excellent impression. Compared with average-run Americans, these British sailors have a freshness about them and an individual distinctness. These people have not spent their lives running, and they have not been run over by life. One wonders whether America could continue to exist when we stop running. There is a streak of extremism in us: we either run or do not move at all. To stop running might edge most of us toward inertness and stagnation.

June 15

Danish ship at Pier 31. More meat from New Zealand. I have been feeling quite well the last couple of days—light of heart and alert.

Diehl's book on Byzantium is pleasant and sometimes stimulating. Here and there Byzantium reminded me of today's America. He quotes a sixth-century writer about the popular preoccupation with chariot races in the Hippodrome which inflamed men's souls to inordinate heights of passion: "Should the green charioteer take the lead, some are in despair; should the blue overtake him half the city is in mourning. People with no personal interest in the matter utter frantic imprecations; those who have suffered nothing feel grievously wounded." He adds, "The most serious men declared that without theatre and Hippodrome life would have been virtually joyless." The Emperor himself took sides in the contest as passionately as anyone.

I have always wondered whether it is vital for a society that all its members should have some common subjects in which they are equally interested and in which they all have some expertise. In Byzantium the common subjects were theology and chariot races. In this country they are machines and sports.

On the way home, in the bus, it struck me that Little Eric is the only human being I have grown onto—that the relation between us is that of a graft. Many elements went into the making of this graft, not the least of which is that he is my namesake. The fact is also important that he is still to me, after 2½ years, a new human being—a newly arrived visitor on this planet. Now and then I feel like asking him how he likes this country.

June 16

In this morning's *Chronicle* Tito is quoted as saying of the Chinese Communists that in attacking Jugoslavia they are using "such insulting language that even Marx and Lenin, if they could hear it, would turn over in their graves." Unintentionally, Tito is here pointing at Marx and Lenin as paragons of rudeness. Good manners are inconceivable without a degree of objectivity, and the give and take of compromise. He who clings with all his might to an absolute truth fears compromise more than the devil. He throttles the soft amenities which would dovetail him with others, and blur his uncompromising stance. Thus it happens that when a faith loses its potency rudeness often serves as a substitute.

June 17

To Stockton with Lili and the boy. The child is utterly charming and obnoxious by turns. It was a good day and a long one. We started at seven in the morning and came back at seven-thirty in the evening. Lili is herself again, which means that she is genuine, and incredibly forbearing. The boy was hard to handle—he spites or humors me as the spirit moves him. On the way back Lili turned, on the spur of the moment, into the road which goes to the top of Mount Diablo. My fear was that we had not gas enough. I shall remember vividly the drive up because of my unceasing alarm until we returned to the main highway.

I spent about $25, and they were well spent. It was the first time in months that I have gotten out of the city. The country, though scorched by summer, was pleasing to the eye. The yellows were satin, and the greens of a metallic quality and of a dozen shades.

June 22

Nine and three-quarter hours on the *Hawaiian Wholesaler* in Encinal. Steady grind but the loads moved slowly. A good bunch. I felt better at 6 P.M. than I did in the morning.

I spoke with a tall Montenegrin whom I call Negus. He is Communist in his sympathies, bitter about this country, chock-full of grievances, but we get along. I asked him how many years ago Stephen Dushan lived. He answered correctly: about six hundred years ago. I felt I could discuss with this barely literate Montenegrin some of the things I have learned from Diehl's *Byzantium*. I pointed out that the Bible was translated into Serbian, Bulgarian, and Russian before it was translated into German, French, and English. How come? Because in the West the Catholic Church was an independent power, an imperial power, and it did not want to see the formation of national churches which might be promoted by a translation of the Bible into common speech. On the other hand, the Byzantian church, being under the thumb of the Emperor, was interested solely in the Christianization of the warlike barbarians, and this could be effected more readily by the formation of national churches.

Eventually, national churches came into being also in the West, and nations crystallized around these churches. This is a significant point: The compact churchly organization of Christianity promoted nation formation, while Islam, being without a churchly organization, could not supply a nucleus for national crystallization. This suggests that compact Communist parties rather than promote internationalism may in the long run foster nationalist separatism.

He was listening attentively and shaking his head, but I had no way of telling whether he got the hang of what I said. When I finished he shook my hand and said: "It is always wonderful to talk with you." Of one thing I am sure: He will always remember, and brag about it, that the Bible was translated into Serbian long before it was translated into English—that Serbian literature is more ancient than English literature.

Lili and the boy have been on my mind all these days. I am following a policy of restraint: to see them only once a week. I must not acquire the habit of seeing them too often. I am going to die alone, and it is too late in life to start feeling lonely.

The kink in my side is still there, but it did not prevent me from doing a day's work. It has slowed down my gait, and I tend to bend to one side as I walk, but I don't feel uncomfortable.

June 23

The kink in my back is gone. Yesterday's work did it. The world looks clean and fresh after last night's rain. I have a long list of chores to do, and I am just getting ready to clean my room. Before starting I read the last few pages of *Byzantium.* I cannot tell as yet what I got out of the book. It corrected my view of the Byzantine Empire as a stagnant body. It needs vigor to last a thousand years.

5 P.M. Spent a hectic day getting things done. Now I am caught up. After a meal of lettuce salad and pea soup I sit down to drink a glass of tea and read. I happened to read the latest issue of the *Nation.* Suddenly I threw it away as a distasteful thing (whining, self-righteous, carping, petulant) and turned to a new travel book by Lord Kinross. This is a continuation of his book on the interior of Asia Minor.

7 P.M. The second Kinross book, so far as I read, is inferior to the first. Since I am in the mood to make it easy for myself I switched to another book—a delightful one. It is a book of letters written by an American woman who lived in Jerusalem 1953-54. It is a warm, sensitive, honest book. My first reaction is: What delightful people Americans are. I ought perhaps to say fine people. And saying this I reflect that I certainly am not an American. Under similar circumstances I would have been neither delightful nor fine. Here she is among total strangers and she does not carp or criticize, or betray the least trace of bad temper. The American's capacity for fraternization is a noble feature, a true foretaste of the

brotherhood of man. The book is *Letters from Jerusalem* by Mary Clawson. I shall probably sit up all night reading it.

June 24

I spent five hours (8-1) with Lili and the boy. Lili is wholly herself and a joy to be with. The boy is of absorbing interest to me. Though almost three years old he is yet to me a stranger—someone from another world come to live among us. He is tireless, fairly clumsy, and can be wonderfully affectionate.

In the afternoon the doorbell rang and a young man came up. He is working for the U.S. Information Office, and seemed intelligent and alert. We talked about the backward countries and how terribly handicapped an American is when dealing with them. It is hopeless to try to win the weak over to our side. We have no ideology to impart, no faith to propagate, and no pride we can share with others. We have much to give in skills and tangible things. We can teach backward people how to work and how to be efficient. But no backward country could ever identify itself with America and be won over completely to our side. How strange it is! The whole world is imitating us, is becoming Americanized, yet the countries that become like us tend to resent us. And the reason is that we cannot win the intellectuals, the men of words, the self-appointed spokesmen who stand between us and the millions we try to help. All the rudeness and biting comes from the intellectuals, and we must have the dossier of the intellectual from way back at our finger tips—from his first appearance as a scribe with the invention of writing. An American is more truly of the masses than any intellectual anywhere, and he can benefit the masses more than any intellectual could do.

June 25

Nine hours on the Pope & Talbot *Leader* at Howard Street. Nothing much to do all day, but the last hour was hectic—sewer pipe. Since I didn't sleep enough last night I feel tired.

I saw today a gentle-spoken longshoreman whom I have not seen for over a year. He works most of the time on the Oakland side of the bay. He is afflicted with an eruption round his nose. It has become much worse now. The flesh of his face is being eaten away, and his eyes are lusterless and lost amidst the expanse of decomposition. I told him how glad I was to see him. It is difficult to visualize the suffering of the man, particularly his thoughts as he rises in the morning.

July 1

Nine hours on the *Flying Enterprise* at Pier 34. A busy day but not unpleasant. The work though steady was not rushed.

Both morning and evening are now cold and wet, but the middle of the day has a warm brilliance. The bay as seen through the huge open door in the back of the dock seemed a fairyland. I don't think a landscape can come into a room through a window. It can come in only through a door.

The fact that I accomplish little when I take time off disqualifies me as a writer. I do have an original idea now and then. If I hang on with all my might, I eventually put together a few thousand words. It may take a year. I lack a flow of words. The most crucial words are never at my service. I have to search and recruit them anew every time.

July 2

Followed the *Flying Enterprise* to Oakland. An easy day in warm weather. A discussion with several Slavonians on the

13

relative merits of America and the Old Country. What it comes to is that this is not a country for the old. After twenty some years in America, these Slavonians are still homesick for their native village. They are excellent workers—skilled and conscientious. They look healthy, and young for their age. But the American tempo grates on them. They talk of the ease and the slowness back home, and how men over fifty no longer work but sit around talking and sipping coffee, letting their children take care of things, and remain hale till they are eighty or more. Actually, none of these Slavonians would be happy if they went back. A few tried and rushed back to America. I mentioned the fact. One of them said: "It may be so, but it will be our greed that will drag us back."

Early this morning on my way to work I felt a burning pain in the arms. It seemed to me for a moment that had I been without this pain I would have been wholly happy. In a moment like this I realize how lucky we are when nothing at all—good or bad—happens to us.

July 3

Worked the same ship the same place. A cold wet gale is just now blowing outside and the world is lost in thick fog.

More talk with the Slavonians. As I said, they are extremely competent people. I found that most of them built their own houses, have small vegetable gardens, and each has a well-appointed workshop in the basement. I cannot see how people of their kind back in the Old Country need a totalitarian government to tell them what to do. Even the most perfect central planning could not achieve anything approaching what these people manage to do on their own.

Returning to the talk about the Old Country, I remarked that there is nothing to prevent them from getting together and re-creating somewhere in California a replica of the village they came from. They are all of them well off, and it should not be impossible to obtain the required financing from a bank or even from a government agency. One of them said: "It can't be done. The air here is not clear. Even in the mountains there is gas and smoke. In the Old Country the air is sweet."

July 3

Nine hours on the Chilean ship *Almagro* in Encinal. Quite a number of people on the Chilean ship look like intellectuals. I don't think they are passengers. In several Latin-American countries the intellectuals go not only into teaching and the civil service but also into the army. This is probably one reason why army officers are meddling in government. It could be that lack of employment prompted some intellectuals to become sailors on merchant ships.

I am reading *An American in India* by Saunders Redding. The author is an American Negro sent by the State Department to India. It is a perplexing and depressing book. A sick man writing about sick people. When facing the most preposterous questions and defamatory insinuations, he remains speechless. He tells us that he identifies himself with America, yet here is a man of words without words. The whole performance leaves a bad taste in my mouth. I suspect that for an American audience this is probably the most anti-Indian book they could read.

July 7

Same ship, same place. Six hours. In the morning I took the key-system bus to Encinal. As I walked down the several blocks from the bus stop to the docks I was impressed by the gardens in front of the houses. The houses, of average size, are fairly old, yet in excellent shape. The people living here are mostly workingmen. The sight of the gardens and houses turned my mind to the question of maintenance. It is the capacity for maintenance which is the best test for the vigor and stamina of a society. Any society can be galvanized for a while to build something, but the will and the skill to keep things in good repair day in, day out are fairly rare. At present, neither in the Communist countries nor in the newly created nations is there a pronounced capacity for maintenance. I wonder how true it is that after the Second World War the countries with the best maintenance were the first to recover. I am thinking of Holland, Belgium, and Western Germany. I don't know how it is in Japan. The Incas had an intense awareness of maintenance. They assigned whole villages and tribes to keep roads, bridges and buildings in good repair. I read somewhere that in ancient Rome a man was disqualified as a candidate for office because his garden showed neglect.

Saunders Redding's book is worth reading for its detailed recording of the talk of the Indian intellectuals both young and old. He reproduces minutely their arguments, rudeness, sarcasm, and self-righteousness. Since he seldom essayed a rebuttal his recording comes out sharp and forceful.

July 8

Finished the job on the Chilean ship *Almagro* at Pier 19. Ten hours. The work was easy but I feel quite weary at the end of the day. My weariness generates in me bad temper, but this shows itself only when I return to my room. After a glass of hot tea and some fruit, and particularly after writing a few lines, the irritation fades more or less.

Saunders Redding's book is a fascinating puzzle. His tongue-tiedness in the face of the crudest slanders and insults might be merely a continuation of the technique he perfected in the face of slights and insults in his own America. I doubt whether the ability to identify oneself with America is proportionate to one's acceptance by fellow Americans. There is an intense patriotism among the rejected—inmates of prisons, and migratory workers living on the edge of subsistence. The question is whether a Negro intellectual can feel himself truly and wholly an American. I don't know. The Negroes I know can be fiercely American. I once heard a Negro longshoreman, while observing a Hindu crew on a British ship, pour forth his scorn on the way poor people are treated in the cold world outside America.

As I said, the fact that Redding rarely hit back or even argued enabled him to record faithfully all that the Indian intellectuals threw at him, and by doing so he has produced the most anti-Indian book I know of.

July 9

I had several good hours with Lili and the boy. He is growing up fast and is becoming reasonable. He ate a frozen boysenberry tart which he greatly enjoyed. For the first time I saw him attack food methodically—eating first the loose berries on the plate and, after cleaning them up, tackling the tart. I savor being with him the way I savor food and drink. Lili is still herself, and nothing can go wrong. Everything we do is adequate, everything we say meaningful, everything we see memorable.

July 10

There is something in the air. You come to expect America to fail whether it be in the launching of a satellite, the exhibition at the Brussels Fair, the intervention in the Near East, the revival of the slumping economy. We are not in the van, and we are not going anywhere in a hurry. To those in the van much is forgiven; their blemishes and shortcomings are temporary, since they are growing and rushing into the future. But to those who are not going anywhere, the present (made up of vulgarity, senseless haste, juvenility, dishonesty) is all there is. You are aware all of a sudden that the country is in dire need of an exceptional leader. The need is an unhealthy symptom.

July 12

Pier 38. One o'clock start. The five-hour shift (1-6) passed without the least strain.

Reading Ivan Bunin's little book *Memories and Portraits* reinforced my conviction that life with writers, artists, and intellectuals in general is most likely to be irritating and unpleasant. Wherever these people come together the air will be charged with envy and malice. It could be that the air thus charged stimulates the creative flow. Yet what a strained and miserable life it would be!

July 14

Finished the job at Pier 38. Nine hours. Though the same work and company, I felt less weary this evening than last. The reason: eight hours' sleep last night, and a good hot lunch today. Yesterday (Sunday) all the restaurants were closed and I had two sandwiches and a piece of pie for lunch.

This morning, some item in the paper started me thinking on the cause of British defeatism. Quite a number of people in Britain seem to envisage the defeat of the West and even the occupation of Britain by Soviet troops. I wonder whether this defeatist prognostication is born of a secret wish to see the defeat and decline of the whole West. The decline of the British Empire seems to be having a more demoralizing effect on British intellectuals (who were supposedly anti-imperialist) than on businessmen. One wonders how much of "the unbought grace of life" of the British intellectual was derived from the fact that British red covered half of the map of the world. They have seen this map from childhood and known the axiom that the British are natural rulers. The British do not want to decline by themselves. They wish to see their own decline as part of a general, natural process.

July 15

5 A.M. It is wonderfully good that I don't have to go to work. A four-day stretch of work gives a special flavor to a free morning. Come to think of it: no particular place or particular day has ever had a special flavor for me. No homesickness for a place, and no looking forward to a holiday.

The situation in Iraq is not clear. Yesterday five thousand marines landed near Beirut. No one knows how the Russians will react. The idea occurred to me that the present confused goings-on in the Near East made good sense to members of Jehovah's Witnesses. According to them, all that is happening in the world at present is a prelude to the battle of Armageddon which will take place on the plain of Jezreel. The return of the Jews to Israel has for its chief purpose the readying of the battlefield. The kibbutzim which now dot the plain of Jezreel are clearing and leveling the ground, and draining the swamps. Movements of troops, whether in the frozen expanse of Russia or in the heart of America, are preliminary stages in the unfolding of the drama. Yesterday's landing of five thousand marines is a meaningful development. I wonder how many hypotheses which make sense in nuclear physics are more valid than the meaningful hypothesis of Jehovah's Witnesses.

July 20

I have just returned from a union meeting. The discussion about the newly instituted eight-hour shift was as intelligent and absorbing as any I have heard. Several of the speakers, though plain longshoremen, would not have been out of place as delegates to the United Nations or as representatives at difficult negotiations of whatever nature. Details of organization fascinate the average American, and dealing with them brings out his subtle originality. Could this organizational intelligence be effective in science or philosophical speculations?

July 22

Seven and a half hours on the *Lurline* at Pier 35. The depression of spirit which weighed on me last night continues. I slept badly, and felt sleepy all day.

It is questionable whether total integration and removal of discrimination would cure the American Negro of that which ails him, and leave him without a grievance. A Negro minority in a white world could perhaps never become wholesome. In our union the Negro has total equality. There is no discrimination in the assignment of jobs, in earnings, and in elections to office. There are many Negro dispatchers, and a Negro business agent. There are Negroes in the interunion leadership. Considering that most of them are recent arrivals, and hence low in seniority, they have achieved much without having to fight for it. Yet when you hear them talk at our meetings you would think that our union is the darkest South. The Negro living in a white world hates his black skin, and probably agrees with the prevailing prejudice against him. But there are remarkable exceptions. I know several Negroes on the waterfront who as workers and human beings have no match. They are gentle, quiet, conscientious, and highly competent. I would give much to have their life histories—how they managed to go through life without being tainted and blemished.

August 4

Five hours on the *Mikagesan Maru* at Pier 23. I did some composing during the short shift. The reason for today's composing was partly that we had hardly anything to do, since it was all heavy lifts, and partly that I had nothing to read.

It is important that I should note the difficulty and pain I experience in writing. It is incredible how vague is my memory of past difficulties. It is only now, when I am beginning to go through it again, that there is a revival of faded memories. Since the publishing of a couple of books I have been cast in the role of a writer and, without being aware of the utter absurdity of it, I have come to expect things to flow out of my finger tips. The truth is that I have to hammer out each sentence, and must hang on to an idea for ages if aught worthwhile is to be written.

Last evening I sat down at the table to write and could make no headway at all. The irritation was such that I had to dress and get out of my room. I drifted to a cheap movie and saw an old Western (*The Far Horizon*). It was eleven before I went to bed and I was up at four-thirty.

August 15

Nine hours on the Dutch ship *Batjan.* As easy a day as one could wish and no sort of unpleasantness. Still the depression this evening is as black as yesterday. I must face the fact that the chief reason for the depression is that I cannot compose.

August 16

Still on the *Batjan* at Pier 23. Today I somehow managed to compose and make some progress on "Intellectuals as School-masters." In Jewish history between the return from the Babylonian captivity and the destruction of the second temple the schoolmasters prevailed against kings, nobles, and priests. The result was a school possessing a nation rather than a nation possessing a school. In China, too, during the period of the contending states, the schoolmen were on the march. Confucius, Mo Ti, and their disciples felt themselves qualified as rulers. The schoolmaster Mo Ti organized his disciples into an army of experts in all departments of government. In Greece, schoolmaster Plato maintained that cities will never have rest until schoolmasters become kings. All through the ages schoolmasters seem to have had the delusion that they could order society as readily as they could a classroom. But it is probably the twentieth century that will be seen in retrospect as the golden age of the schoolmaster.

In all contemporary mass movements schoolmasters played a vital and often leading role. I am willing to bet that more than half of the leaders in Africa are ex-schoolmasters. In the Nazi movement grammar-school teachers played a prominent and fateful role. Now and then I am inclined to think that the passion to teach, which is far more powerful and primitive than the passion to learn, is a factor in the rise of mass movements. For what do we see in the Communist world? Half of the globe has been turned into a vast schoolroom with a thousand million pupils at the mercy of a band of maniacal schoolmasters.

August 17

Still at Pier 23. Nine hours. Fishing fever has seized many of the people working on this ship. The striped bass are running, and they have been catching real big ones. The result was that half of the time we were short-handed on a big pile of drums. The strain and the irritation combined to make it an unpleasant day. Of course, I didn't write a line.

August 24

Finished loading the *Hawaiian Packer*. The remarkable thing is that I am less tired after a six-day stretch of fairly hard work than I have often been after a one-day job.

What bothers me is that for the first time in my life I am becoming a regular worker, and what's more I am beginning to feel like one. I wonder whether my preoccupation with the role of the intellectual, and my antagonism toward him, have driven me to act the typical workingman.

During the day I got to thinking about the dovetailing and mutuality of inclinations. This came up in connection with the intellectual's need for pride. Being without an unequivocal sense of usefulness and worth, the intellectual has a vital need for pride, which he usually derives from an identification with some compact group, be it a nation, a church, or a party. The idea of a chosen people has been an invention of intellectuals rather than of domineering men of action. But the promotion of a compact, centralized social body not only satisfies the intellectual's need for pride but also offers him opportunities for leading, directing, supervising, managing, and planning—pursuits tailored to the needs and talents of the scribe from the first invention of writing.

August 25

Eight hours on the Norwegian ship *Evanger* at Pier 41. The cargo was cocoa beans and coffee. It was hard work part of the time, but I had a good partner. I began to write the introduction to *Men of Words*. It should be brief.

Just now I am stuck with the beginning of Part 2. I need information about the earliest examples of written literature in Sumer, Egypt, and China.

August 27

Eight hours on the same ship. Steady grind all day long, and I had neither the time nor the inclination to write a line.

In the morning on the bus, I heard a Negro longshoreman argue that the "No Smoking" signs are put up by the fire insurance companies. Pretty soon they'll have "No Smoking" signs inside the house, even in the bedroom. In other countries people smoke wherever they please, but here the insurance companies are running things.

I haven't had a good look at the bay all day. The feeling of being rushed drains the capacity for savoring things.

In the morning I read an article by Max Nomad on "Masters Old and New." Writing in 1937, he clearly discerns the intelligentsia as the coming elite in both capitalist and non-capitalist countries. But the article is without a hint of the intellectual's role in history, and the significance of his dramatic comeback in the twentieth century.

August 28

Eight hours on the same ship. We follow the ship tomorrow to Alameda. The hard work during the last three days is affecting my stomach. Something gets tied up in a knot inside me when I strain my guts. I shall try to straighten it out tonight by drinking hot tea and relaxing.

August 29

Finally finished the ship. Eight and a half hours in Alameda. I am weary and on edge. I must slow down or even stop work for a week.

I must get hold of a biography of Bentham. His transition from a preoccupation with the all-seeing eye (panopticon) to the promotion of the general welfare is an instance of the intimate connection between the intellectual's idealism and his innermost craving for a role of supervision. (Vision & Supervision.)

September 1

I just read the introduction to *Men of Words.* It is not bad. I also copied Sections 8 to 11. I have so far forty pages of manuscript. The thing is crude and fragmented, but it is a beginning.

September 3

Eight hours on the *Arizona Maru* at Pier 24. An easy day, and I am off tomorrow. My head worked in spasms. The beginning of

Part 2 must tackle the problem of the optimal milieu for literature. I shall trace the chain of events which led to the appearance of written literature in Egypt, Sumer, Palestine, Greece, and China. But the main thing is to outline the conditions optimal for literary creativeness.

After all, the chief value of history is not that it helps us understand the present or decipher the future but that it furnishes us clues concerning the manner in which man is affected by his natural and social environment. We cannot experiment with humanity, but history is a record of how man reacted under a variety of conditions.

September 4

I have said it again and again: the only thing that will cure the Negro's chronic ills is that the Negro community perform something that will win it the admiration of the world. Yet it is difficult to see what this something might be. A Negro revolt in Mississippi; a desperate battle to the last man, a Negro Alamo. Or an excellent Negro school for song and dance. Or an excellent trade school. Or a model organization for mutual help. It is the slow, hard way, and the indications are that the Negro will not take it. He would rather derive pride from an identification with the achievements of colored races elsewhere. Yet I doubt whether even a triumphant Ghana could ever be to the Negro in America what Israel has been to the Jews.

The crucial question is whether the Negro will ever give up his alibi of discrimination. You do not give up the imperishable advantage of an alibi for the short-lived exhilaration of achievement. There is trouble ahead. For the less justified the Negro's alibi the more passionately will he cling to it, and the louder will he voice his grievances.

Were I a genuine American I would believe in the possibility of the automatic absorption of twenty million Negroes into the body of American life; that almost overnight, without special effort or an intermediate phase, the Negro in America can become a human being first and only secondly a Negro.

September 26

Seven and a half hours discharging cargo at Pier 17. It was hot but work did not seem irksome. One of the reasons is that I had a good night's sleep, and my partner (Juan Gonzales) though not much of a worker is a pleasant person to be with.

In the morning, while eating breakfast, it occurred to me that the equivalent of a Khrushchev in the West is to be found not among the politicians but the businessmen. A Communist regime is capitalism gone berserk. It is incredible how many insights one obtains when viewing a ruling Communist party as a company of merchant adventurers lodged in the body of a backward country.

During the day a winch driver I know only by sight came over to talk. He started out with the union but immediately passed over to his own affairs. He must have been married for a long time since he has two grandchildren. His wife is now partly paralyzed, and as he talked I could sense the despair and bitterness simmering inside him. The woman must have been slovenly, lazy, and self-centered even while she was well, and now paralyzed she is a millstone round his neck.

September 29

What is the optimal milieu for creativeness in literature, art, music, etc.? It is a milieu which rewards excellence. Cosimo the Elder reverenced talent the way the pious reverence saints. When Arab civilization was at its height, the Ommiad caliphs gave poets and scholars precedence over officials, and some of them were made governors of provinces. To Louis XIV a good sentence was a major achievement.

In an optimal milieu there is considerable leisure. Where people are engrossed in some feverish pursuit so that they are neither bored, nor dream dreams, nor nurse grievances, creativeness will be anemic.

Finally, an optimal milieu is one in which the creative are in close intercourse with each other—hating, loving, envying, admiring; where faces flush, hearts flutter, and minds swell with the passion to rival and emulate.

September 3

The Embarcadero Freeway is being built rapidly, yet one rarely sees more than three workingmen on the job. There are, of course, more than three, but the organization of the work is such that no one stands around. The same holds true on other jobs. Though it would be difficult to prove that the American workingman is the best in the world, it is nevertheless true that the American way of doing things is determined largely by the American workingman's attitude toward work.

I do not know how it is with workingmen elsewhere, but I cannot see an American workingman fitting in and feeling at home anywhere outside this country.

October 1

Eight hours on the *Wonorato* at Pier 23. My partner was the old Slavonian with the big nose and squinting eyes. He has a chip on his shoulder, but his aggressiveness is actually defensive. We got to talking about the achievements of the different nationalities. He said: "You heard about the Slavonian inventor Nikola Tesla? He was greater than Edison, but he remained poor because he was a foreigner. When Edison was trying to make an electric bulb he asked Tesla whether it could be done. Tesla answered in Slavonian: 'Mazda,' which means 'maybe.' This is why they have the word *mazda* on the electric bulbs."

He also told me of a Slavonian longshoreman who went to the old country and just returned. Among the stories he tells is the following one: He was standing on the sidewalk in some town watching a gang of pipefitters at work. They guessed he was an American and one of them asked, "What would they pay us an hour for this kind of work in America?" He answered: "They would not give you five cents."

October 3

It is funny that on my days off I don't feel like keeping the diary.

Today I worked eight hours sorting cargo at Pier 29. It was steady grind, but we had a good bunch.

Yesterday I received a letter from an editor of the *Saturday Evening Post* offering me $2,500 for an article on fanaticism. I shall not answer until I have an article to send him. It won't do to rehash the old stuff.

This morning I happened to think of the possibility that a virulent outburst of fanaticism may precede the death of a faith. Southern fanaticism on the issue of slavery was at its height when slavery became untenable, and the same is true of the present segregationist fervor. The fanaticism of the Crusades preceded the coming of the Renaissance, and the religious fervor of the Thirty Years' War was followed by the skepticism of the seventeenth and eighteenth centuries. It is also true that the rabid chauvinism of the second quarter of the twentieth century is followed by a considerable cooling of the nationalist spirit in the West. The question is how fast do burning problems burn themselves out.

October 4

Four hours at Pier 35 on the *Monterey*. We had about a couple of hours of steady going. The rest of the time we stood around, and I began to feel weary and sleepy.

I spent part of the afternoon in bed. The resolution before going to bed was to finish reviewing the last daybook,* something I have put off for weeks. Yet just now I am leafing through Volume I of Durant's *Story of Civilization*. I shall take a shower, go out to eat, and later spend the evening on the daybook.

Today I caught myself misreading words, again and again. I wonder whether it is my tiredness or a new defect of vision.

11:45 P.M. Worked some on the daybook. Much of the stuff has faded from my memory—particularly the Irish influence as a factor in Australia's attitude toward work. But Rommel's *Papers* drew me away from that. I picked up the book in the library this evening and can't let go of it.

October 5

Eight hours at Pier 39. A pleasant day. The work was steady but not strenuous, and the company good. It is not work but the unpleasantness that sometimes goes with it that makes a day wearisome. Haste, argument, friction of any sort result in fatigue and dejection. I would work five hours rather than argue five minutes.

In the morning before turning to work I happened to think of the outcry of the intellectuals when the bay bridges were being built during the depression. The intellectual sees man's handiwork as a defacement. His glorification of nature stems partly from his deprecation of practical achievements. He does not object to monuments, statues, and non-utilitarian structures. The fact that bridges and freeways are utilitarian prompts him to see them as a defilement. With common people it is the other way around: they see man's work as an enhancement of nature. On the whole, common people have a better opinion of mankind than do the educated. If it is true as Bergson says that "the human nature from which we

---

* A notebook I carry around with me wherever I go. When it is full, I review it. Any quotation or thought worth preserving is copied out.

turn away is the human nature we discover in the depths of our being" then the intellectual is in a hell of a fix. There is no getting away from it: education does not educate and gentle the heart.

October 6

Cleaned the room, took care of the laundry, went down to the hall to sign up and pay dues. The rest of the time I just fiddled around. In the evening I went to see a movie.

Lili returned and brought over the boy for a few minutes. He has become demonstratively affectionate. At three years he has an astounding range of understanding and feeling. His capacity for utmost remembrance and utmost forgetting is a puzzle. He forgets his grievances and hurts in a jiffy. He cannot be inflated durably nor can he be humbled and crushed. Yet he has a phenomenal memory for sights and sounds. He knows most of the letters of the alphabet, the names of a hundred animals, can easily identify any number of melodies, and knows quite a number of nursery rhymes by heart. He learns rapidly. But, as I said, he forgets in a flash many things, even those which caused him pain enough to make him cry.

October 7

Finally finished reviewing the daybook. There are no more than three or four seminal ideas in the whole thing. The one I like best is why the Incas did not invent writing.

This morning on my way back from breakfast I spent some time in the City Hall. I must take Little Eric to see the building and give him a feel of monumentality.

I am still tired, and I begin to realize that the cure for tiredness is not rest.

October 8

Eight hours on a Japanese ship at Ninth Avenue loading onions. The heat and sweat have left me limp. I can't even read, let alone write. There is no use changing course ten days before the vacation. It is conceivable that thoughts are dammed up within me, and once the flow of words starts all will be well. I have had the feeling for months that steady work has settled a thick carpet of dust over my mind—a dust bowl.

Before starting work this morning I wondered what effect the increased sale of foreign cars—favored and promoted mainly by intellectuals—has had on advertisers and magazine editors. If the intellectual can set the tone and prevail against powerful business interests then he is a factor that must be taken into account. His tastes must be catered to. This is perhaps one of the reasons that the *Saturday Evening Post* is printing highbrow articles and is paying extravagantly for them.

October 13

This has been the sixth straight day of work, and I probably feel more chipper and limber now than when I started last Wednesday. Chances are if I went on working day after day I might notice cycles of tiredness, a curve of fatigue. I might get over my tiredness even as I work. How my mind would fare is hard to say. Long periods of rest have not had a stimulating effect. Unless I have my teeth into a subject, and a body of manuscript to rethink and rewrite, there is no guarantee that leisure will be productive. I am even afraid to try it and find out. Have I a subject right now? I know that the intellectual is not it. Nor is it fanaticism. Chances are that the intellectual, the true believer, mass movements, etc., are facets of a larger problem. None of these topics can stir and excite me just now. It could be that all my life I have had a single, central preoccupation, and I still do not know what it is.

October 15

It is not usually the overpowering experience which sets off a flow of thought. Some trivial incident or even a mere word may pull the trigger. Hence the fact that a second-rate book may be more stimulating than a masterpiece.

Christopher Dawson in *Dynamics of World History* pictures H. G. Wells as a schoolmaster to whom statesmen are no more than a number of troublesome and occasionally incendiary schoolboys. The intellectual's taste for making history and his penchant for immortality add up to a species of insanity. How strange that both society as a business corporation and society as a school are likely to be tyrannies.

October 16

Eight hours on a German ship (the *Bamberg?)* at Pier 26. I still wonder whether the German republican flag (black, red, and yellow) grates on the average German as it did after the First World War. Considering the present absorption of the Germans in private affairs and their determination to cultivate each his garden it probably matters little what the flag is. It will be a momentous turning point in the affairs of Europe if it be true that the Germans have wearied of their nationalism. Of course, the German tendency toward fanaticism may find a new dangerous outlet, though I cannot see what it could be.

All day long I mused vaguely and apprehensively about the coming vacation. I must guard myself against isolation. I shall be seeing Lili and the boy every Tuesday. I have just received two invitations for dinner, and I have to meet the editors and journalists from Southeast Asia. The main thing is not to take myself seriously.

October 17

Finished the German ship at Pier 26. Seven hours. On the way home I was overcome by a fit of drowsiness. This is surprising since I had a good night's sleep and the work during the day was fairly easy.

I just read several thoughts I had copied last night. It is surprising how many words I had missed. After a day's work I find that I can sketch a train of thought in bold strokes, but I can't copy faultlessly nor can I express myself with precision.

October 18

Eight hours at Pier 29 on a Luckenbach ship. I am replacing a regular dockman in Rekula's gang. Most of the gang are Finns, and when I am with them they stuff me full of Finnish words. Today I learned to count up to ten, and a dozen words or so concerning the weather, ships, and the work.

It occurred to me during the day that in my present state of weariness I ought not to make any plans. My mind is not in good shape. After catching my breath and spending some time with myself I may be able to gauge things and decide what to do. Tomorrow is my last day of work. Perhaps for the first time in my life I am looking forward to a vacation.

I seem to be afraid to make an outline of what I am going to say to the intellectuals from Southeast Asia next Thursday. I ought to speak about the American worker—his readiness to work, his skill, his ability to get things done with a minimum of supervision, and his attitude toward the pencil pushers.

October 19

Finished the job at Pier 29. It was a very pleasant job. The Finns are the salt of the earth. The fact that my vacation starts tomorrow settled everything for me, else I would have probably trailed with the gang for weeks.

What surprises me again and again in this country is the rapidity with which an experience is savored and exhausted. Each new fashion, vogue, and attitude is pushed up the hill with utter abandon, and once at the top it is allowed to roll back and into the ashcan. The senselessness of it is monumental.

It has happened to me several times: just when it seemed that I had lost the aptitude to grasp and hold a whole train of thought, there followed a period of rapid development.

October 20

5 A.M. Concerning fanaticism in awakening Asia: If you want people to work for little or nothing you have to infect them with fanaticism. Fervor is a substitute for skill and also for capital. When a poor country wants to modernize itself in a hurry, it must know how to induce its people to work for words. Hence the vital role "men of words" play in the awakening of stagnant societies.

Thinking in my case is like sluicing poor placer dirt. You must trap every flake of gold if you are to get anything. The final lump is not a nugget but a "button" made up of innumerable flakes each so slight that it floats.

I am still full of the pleasure I savored while working two days with the Finns. Usually when I work with people for any length their voices keep hammering inside me after I leave them, and I feel like shaking them out of my head. With the Finns it is the other way around—the aftertaste is extremely pleasant, and you allow it to linger on.

This country seems to be undergoing a decisive transformation. I may be wrong but I detect a change in tempo, a letting go of the thundering, gaudy, relentless juggernaut. One of the results of this transformation is that the country is becoming a better place for the old. Up to now the old felt out of place—useless, unwanted, a nuisance to themselves and others. Now there is a mood for enjoying leisure. People do not feel guilty and dejected when they cease working. Axel and Ole, whom I saw while working at Pier 26, looked relaxed. They have been retired for over a year, and they seemed at peace with themselves and the world.

This morning, about 7 A.M., I walked through the Golden Gate park. Trees and flowers had sharp shapes in the morning air. The park looked somehow different from what I remembered it. In full daylight the trees blend and all you see is a mass of green against the sky. In the morning you notice the many nuances of green, and how the foliage of each species forms a different pattern: one a mass of crosses, one of circles, and one of sweeping lines!

The first day of my vacation does not seem memorable. I do not feel particularly free, relaxed, or expectant. Tonight I shall go to the union meeting.

12 P.M. Back from the meeting. Had an unpleasant falling-out with Selden. After the meeting we went to have a drink, and he said something about the fact that we are prone to detect in others the faults we hide in ourselves. He said: "I think our union officials are lazy and dishonest. Does this mean that there is in me a tendency toward laziness and dishonesty?" I tried to tell him that such insights are not cut and dried, that a statement of proven facts about the outside world does not reflect an inner situation, and that there are varieties of laziness and dishonesty. I did not tell him that his sin of laziness was in not making the effort to utilize the training he had been given at Stanford, and that his dishonesty manifests itself in crass self-righteousness. Instead, I brought up the subject of pretentiousness. Selden is always surprised that people are not as pretentious as he had expected them to be. Why

does he expect people to be pretentious? I mentioned something I had observed in him the other day. He had read a report about the cost of containerization at Matson Co. and he was telling us about it. Instead of summarizing what he had learned he made the whole thing seem terribly abstruse and complex—something that the average longshoreman could not hope to master. Actually, the morning papers of that day gave a straightforward report on the subject. Even as I spoke I realized that I was being tactless and stupid. Selden needs sympathy and encouragement rather than criticism. He is genuinely convinced that he has not an atom of pretense, dishonesty, or self-seeking and so on. He knows he is perfect. He is convinced that the reason the majority of long-shoremen do not admire him, trust him, and vote for him is that they are stupid, malicious, and dishonest. Criticism could not possibly change his opinions and attitudes. It only embitters him. The best course is to listen to him and get used to his self-righteousness. For all I know, in Selden's present state of mind seeing things as they are might be fatal. He perhaps has to be self-righteous in order to survive. Since I see little of him it should not be a strain on me to be uncritical.

Selden fits Nietzsche's description of the idealist: "A creature who has reasons for remaining in the dark about himself, and who is also clever enough to remain in the dark concerning these reasons."

October 21

8 A.M. This is the second day of my vacation and already I feel as if I had spent a whole month doing nothing. I have forgotten how to rest and not give a damn. Went to sleep last night at three. A book written by a group of German generals kept me up. When I finally went to bed I slept fitfully. Some sort of anxiety is hammering inside me.

October 23

I plumb forgot to write anything yesterday. I went down to Santa Cruz to see Bill Dale. Left 7:30 A.M. and returned 8 P.M. Walked about five miles in the heat through the canyon. It is long since I felt so much a stranger in this world.

Today I have to meet the journalists from Southeast Asia, and it preys on my mind. It seems to me that I shall be carefree when it is over.

6:30 P.M. It was a hell of a meeting with a pack of biting, hissing, crummy intellectuals. I rubbed their noses in dirt. These people came to us to look and learn, but as men-of-words they were contemptuous of our practicalness, and our addiction to acts rather than words. Since America was shaped by the masses it seems to them that we have no civilization at all. I responded with an attack on the sort of civilization they cherish—a civilization shaped and dominated by scribes—and warned them to beware of American influence. For Americanization affects mainly the masses, stiffens their backbone, and infects them with a passion to act on their own, get their full share of the good things of life, and dispense with the tutelage of scribes and clerks. I remembered Saunders Redding, the American Negro in India, and the sort of baiting he had to endure without hitting back. I struck out in all directions. Bill Stucky of the American Press Institute said it was the first time anyone had talked back to them. They had needled and baited everyone from Dulles down. Americans don't know how to be rude to foreigners. I am glad I let them have it.

October 24

2:30 P.M. A hefty chapter in *Men of Words* should deal with the intellectual's attitude toward America.

7:30 P.M. Spent hours in the Mechanics Library. When I returned, my room seemed cheerful and I said "Hello" to the four walls. I am going to boil up some pea soup with Vienna sausages, drink hot tea, and read a book by Van der Post on the Kalahari Desert and the Bushmen.

Many topics have gone stale on me, while others remain fresh. I know that the field of self-awareness is about played out. The origin of the modern Occident has become a somewhat dim subject, perhaps from neglect. The intellectual is still in the center, though I am aware of a deep reluctance to go on with it. The uniqueness of man and the nature of change are subjects I would love to tackle.

During the whole day I have not spoken half a dozen sentences yet I feel as if I had been engaged in an interminable dialogue. The optimal milieu for me is to be surrounded by people and not be part of them.

October 25

I am troubled that I sometimes feel as if I were conferring a favor on people by spending my time with them. It is a puzzle that I should be aware of such a feeling at a time when deep inside me there are dark doubts about my creative potentialities. Acting humbly might help. But the important thing is to find the reason. People do not interest me as much as they did a couple of years ago. Perhaps the weakening of the sexual impulse, too, has rendered people less attractive and interesting.

October 26

I woke up with the idea that it was Monday. It cheered me somewhat to realize that it was not yet. I spent several hours downtown eating breakfast and strolling about.

I wonder how much of the feeling of well-being that I have had now and then during the past two days comes from the book I am reading—Van der Post's *The Lost World of the Kalahari.*

Nothing this man ever writes could be without the excitement of life. And even as he brings to life the landscape, the plants, the animals, and the human beings he also manages to put the quality of himself in every word. You wonder what would happen if he became the absolute ruler of a primitive African state, and how little it would require to change him into an ancient lawgiver, a magician, a healer. His prose though unlabored is genuine poetry. You begin to realize that the chief function of poetry is to use words as charms to evoke life and colors and smells—a sense of joy, of awe, of compassion, and so on.

Yet all the time you know that it is the man and not his words that count. Wherever he puts his foot the earth becomes portentous. It is as if his presence has diverted the elements and forces from their routine pursuits. The whole world is addressing him, and concerning itself with his tastes and intentions.

October 27

Felt lethargic all day. The question is still whether the numbness is temporary or permanent. Working as I did during the past year I have a right to some leisure. Still, the decision to ease up on work when the vacation is over will depend on whether the flow of thinking and writing can be released.

All day I resisted the impulse to get in touch with Lili. Once I do this I shall again have an alibi for not doing anything.

I finished the Van der Post book. I doubt very much whether I would enjoy his fiction. He is so visionary and ethereal when he describes reality that I have to remind myself repeatedly that he is a truthful man reporting what he saw and felt. On the other hand I would like very much to read a history of a remote era written by him—a crucial era such as the birth of cities or the discovery of the mind in Ionia.

I am developing an exaggerated conception of the value of fluency. Actually, the subjects which interest me can be tackled without fluency. Still, you must write if you are to write at all.

October 28

6:30 A.M. One can achieve more in a few fruitful minutes than in months of effort. The same problem which confronts the cultural historian also baffles the individual facing himself. What is it that releases our energies, kindles our mind, illumines our soul, and gives winged words to dim stirrings inside us? Creativeness has both a social and an individual aspect. Flowering and decline are cycles which occur both in the history of a society and in the life span of the individual.

8:30 P.M. Spent a happy afternoon with the boy. I took him downtown to buy him shoes and clothes. There was not the least trace of unpleasantness. He minds me and is always ready with a smile.

I derive a subtle pleasure from the conviction that the world does not owe me anything. I need little to be contented: two good meals a day, tobacco, books that hold my interest, and a little writing every day. This to me is a full life.

The fact sticks out: American businessmen, intellectuals, soldiers, and diplomats can work abroad. But not American workingmen! The only place abroad where an American workingman might feel at ease would be the communal settlements in Israel. The chief reason that the American soldiers who defected to Red China returned home was that they could not ever fit in there as workingmen. Were they intellectuals they would have probably stayed put.

Afterthought: The American gangster, too, can never feel at home abroad.

October 29

I have not worked out in detail the differences between Islam and Christianity. Whereas Christianity, both in the West and in the East, promoted national crystallization, Islam had on the whole a denationalizing effect. Only in Persia, with its awareness of a superior culture and its memories of past glories, did national consciousness persist after conversion to Islam. Both Islam and the Roman Empire were denationalizing agents. Both incorporated the elites everywhere into the conquering ruling class. After two centuries of Islam the bureaucracy and the military were wholly in the keeping of non-Arabs. The bureaucracy, known as "the people of the pen," was largely responsible for the flowering of Islamic culture. The converted masses, too, found pride and fulfillment in Islam. Renan's theory that it was the denationalization caused by the Roman Empire which brought about an increased interest in social problems and a receptivity to new religious movements does not hold true of Islam. Islam seemed to fulfill every need and had a tranquilizing effect. The end result was stagnation.

Compared with Christianity, Islam is almost without inner contradictions—between church and state, profession and performance, the spirit and the flesh. We somehow assume that inner contradictions, if severe enough, may bring about the breakdown of a society or a system. Actually, vigor and creative flow have their source in internal strains and tensions. It is the pull of opposite poles that stretches souls. And only stretched souls make music.

October 30

6:30 A.M. You accept certain unlovely things about yourself and manage to live with them. The atonement for such an acceptance is that you make allowances for others—that you cleanse yourself of the sin of self-righteousness.

1 P.M. Had a beautiful walk with Lili through the park. We wound up at the Cliff House drinking hot rum with butter and lemon. I have missed her and it was like coming home. We got the boy out of school at 11:30 and had hamburgers at Petrini's. I can still savor the taste of a happy morning.

Part of my organic tie with Lili and the boy is a certain prescience. Maybe it is simply familiarity, a knowledge of the landscape: you know what's ahead of you.

October 31

They have been predicting the dire things that would happen to art, literature, and culture in general if the lowbrow masses asserted themselves and imposed their tastes on a society. But could anything equal the inanity and imposture spewed by avant-garde cliques and accepted by self-appointed guardians of our culture?

Eventually the inanities will be swept away by people of talent who will build the new with a sure hand. My feeling is that when talented people who have something to say use the new techniques their work will be accessible even to the uninitiated.

1 P.M. How easy it is to forget a mood or perhaps feelings in general. We can remember an act or something we saw, heard, or smelled, but we cannot remember the feelings of happiness, despair, elation, dejection, etc., unless we have encased them in words.

November 1

I notice wild fluctuations of confidence. Ten minutes after I have finished writing something passably good I wonder how I managed to do it.

A stranger spoke to me on Powell Street. He knew my name and wanted to talk. We went into Compton's and talked for a while over a cup of coffee. He is a typical lesser intellectual: interested in ideas, but without an inkling of what an original idea is. What role do ideas play in his life? They perhaps give him the feeling that he is walking in higher regions, that he is above the noise, stench, and pain of the present. I am quite certain that had I chosen my illustrations from petty everyday life rather than from history and world politics he would have felt it as a desecration. Ideas and words are to him a badge of distinction.

Fair play with others is primarily the practice of not blaming them for anything that is wrong with us. We tend to rub our guilty conscience against others the way we wipe dirty fingers on a rag. This is as evil a misuse of others as the practice of exploitation.

November 2

On Market Street: Two young people with dark glasses, and dressed in slacks. Even after looking closely at them I could not tell whether they were men or women. Has there ever been a time in history when the difference between the sexes became so unaccentuated that it was difficult to tell a man from a woman? Such a leveling of the sexes must involve biological changes. We read about effeminacy in past ages but I doubt whether it meant an effacement of the differences between the sexes.

I watched Negroes going to church. They were well-dressed and prosperous looking—typical middle class. It occurred to me that the real "International" is that of the middle class. Workers are and look different in different countries despite all the talk about the Workers' International. The same is true of aristocrats, intellectuals, and most other human types. But a typical middle-class family looks the same in Tokyo, Timbuctu, or even in Moscow.

And one has the feeling that what we know as "modern times" is closely bound up with this middle-class pattern. Domination by aristocrats, intellectuals, workers, or soldiers will always manifest a return to past eras—to feudalism, the Middle Ages or even the ancient river-valley regime of Egypt and Mesopotamia.

It seems to me that I savor food now more than I did in my middle years, and almost as much as in childhood. I look forward to breakfast as I go to bed, and during the day I think often of supper.

November 3

How hard it is to know what is really happening to us. With the propaganda of the "I" pervading every cell of our being, we cannot see clearly the true reason for what we do or do not do.

Right now I feel upset, weary, and empty. It'll take at least twenty-four hours to restore the simple pattern which alone can give me a sense of peace. I spent the afternoon at Lili's. The Osborne household upsets me. The boy is at his worst with the family around him. The flea-bitten dog irritates me. Finally, not having eaten anything since breakfast, I stuffed myself with Lili's good food, and felt miserable afterward.

It is the last week of my vacation and I have accomplished nothing. The soothing doctrine is that it is an evil thing to expect too much from ourselves and from others. I have a few years ahead of me and they will probably consist of four days' work a week on the waterfront, fragmentary thinking and writing, time and money spent with Lili and the boy. Nothing exciting, hopeful, unexpected, and hardly any growth. But it is a bearable existence.

I'd better write down what happened at the Osbornes' and get it out of my system. Little Eric was in a boisterous mood. He is usually so when he has not had a good nap in the afternoon. At table he sat at my right, and I tried to quiet him down. He got red in the face and shouted at me: "You no belong to the house any-how!" His father across the table had a peculiar smile on his face. This is the most complex household imaginable, with everyone pulling in a different direction. The moods swing wildly from one extreme to the other, and so do the attitudes toward me. A stay in the Osborne house usually depresses me. Yet I love every one of them. In my attitude toward them there is a mixture of warm compassion and irksome annoyance. At some moments I am convinced that I am being drained and bled. I also have now and then a sense of approaching doom. With Selden's somber sulking, Tonia's epilepsy, Lili's spells of thoughtlessness, anything may happen. Steve's hunger for security may be typical of boys his age, but it has a quality of foreboding. Even Little Eric with all his innocence and robustness fills me with unease. He is unusually intelligent and sensitive, and his vehemence is strangely unchild-like. On Halloween night his mother dressed him in motley and started to paint his face. The moment he saw himself in the mirror he began to cry and yell: "I no this; I Eric." I can see a Laurens van der Post entering this household and describing the omens peeping out of every corner.

November 4

At breakfast I worked on a section dealing with the antago-nism between action and creativeness. Usually it is the thwarted impulse toward action that works itself out in creativeness. Sheer inaction does not automatically promote literature, art, music, etc. There has to be a passionate desire for imposing action and an impossibility of realizing it. People thus thwarted tend to become either revolutionaries or writers, artists, etc., depending on a person's natural endowments. Any way you look at it creativeness springs from an inner tension. In addition to the tension there have to be talents. Where there are no talents, tension vents itself in a variety of action.

In the afternoon I took Little Eric to the beach. We walked along the water from Fulton Street to the zoo. The boy is tireless. We wrote letters on the smooth, wet sand. It would take very little to teach him to read. He still does not know what dead means, although he uses the word frequently. We saw two dead sea gulls. We wound up at the Hitchrack restaurant, where we ate and played the jukebox. Lili came at 5:30. By the time she drove me home the boy had fallen asleep.

November 5

9 A.M. I have to buy a hundred things before the vacation ends, but I can't get started. I'll have to break through the blockage and start to spend. I need shoes, a raincoat, a blanket, underwear, and above all a new phonograph. I feel guilty about my reluctance to buy things. Yet there is a deep satisfaction in the awareness that I really need few things to keep me contented.

4:30 P.M. Didn't go anywhere; didn't buy a thing. Thursday and Friday left to try. I'll have to do it if it kills me.

Right now I feel that I could spend the rest of my life in relative inactivity such as I experienced during the past three weeks. I have stifled ambition because I loathe tension. And I have done all I could not to take myself seriously.

The twentieth century is not only the century of the intellectuals but also of women. Women have entered the social arena in both Russia and China. You probably need something like a new race when you start to build a new world. You can create a new race by the genocide of a whole class as Stalin did when he liquidated the most enterprising and civilized segment of the Russian population, and made of Russia a nation of lesser mujiks. The entrance of women on a large scale amounts to the introduction of a new human type. And what excellent material are women for the building of a totalitarian society! Their capacity for blind faith, self-sacrifice, leader worship, and snooping makes them ideal true believers. What a picture: an elite of intellectuals served and guarded by an army of amazons.

November 6

Bought a pair of work shoes, and a comforter for the bed. Both at Sears, Roebuck, and both for the same price—$13.

The vacation is drawing to an end. It is back to work next Monday. I had a real rest. My mind is not in excellent shape, but it has begun to work. The hardest thing is to begin.

November 7

What would life be without coincidences? Actually, all prayers and hopes are a reaching-out for coincidences. Most of the time, too, it is the timely occurrence of chance which gives us the feeling that we are really going somewhere. For all I know, a life is great because it is a crossroad of coincidences.

Where sheer survival is concerned accidents are less decisive in the case of man than in the case of animals. Much of the time, society shields a person against death by accident. But in the shaping of a life, chance and the ability to respond to chance are everything.

The idea that man is a stranger on this planet always excites me. To feel wholly at home in the world is to partake of the nature of an animal. I play with the fancy that some contagion from outer space was perhaps the seed of man. The present fascination with outer space, and the eternal preoccupation with stars, heaven, and God are a sort of homing impulse which draws us back to where we came from.

November 8

The danger is that I may lump all intellectuals into one category. The way to avoid the danger is to start from the antagonism between action and creativeness. Both originate in front of an apparently insurmountable obstacle on the path to imposing action. All intellectuals thirst for grandeur and lordship, all want to make history and become immortal. When they come up against an insurmountable obstacle which denies them their heart's innermost desire there occurs a division: those without outstanding talent will tend to become revolutionaries and reformers. They will agitate, theorize, exhort, plot, and do all they can to undermine and blow up the roadblock athwart their path. The talented divert their thwarted energies into new channels. They, too, are critical of their times. Though they usually neither plot nor agitate against the prevailing dispensation, their discontent colors their work and gives it an undertone of protest. There is probably nothing more sublime than discontent transmuted into a work of art, a scientific discovery, and so on. It is a sublime alchemy.

November 9

Sat up most of the night reading *Sinai Victory* by S.L.A. Marshall. It still remains to be seen what the Israelis could do against a real army. The weakness of Egypt cannot be attributed to Islam. It is rather the result of the sapping of the spirit of the people over many centuries. Crucial, too, is the corruption of the educated segment of the population which supplies most of the officers.

It is raining. It will probably be wet when I get back to work. Though I have accomplished very little, it seems to me that I could go on indefinitely doing what I have been doing during the past three weeks.

November 10

Eight hours on the *Steel Scientist* at Pier 39. It was a pleasant day. The gang was made up mostly of Slavonians I know well. Several members of the gang asked me to stay with them until the man whom I replaced, and who is temporarily crippled, returns. I told them I cannot just now stay with a gang since I don't intend to work more than three days a week.

Today, on the job, I read in the *Reader's Digest* about an American consulting firm that had been invited to Peru to straighten out the affairs of a company that was in trouble. The first thing it did was to fire two-thirds of the pencil pushers, all of them university graduates, who would rather starve than do manual labor. American influence threatens the very existence of these intellectuals. Small wonder that the university students in Lima vented their spite and spittle on Richard Nixon. The standing of the intellectuals in South America is probably higher than anywhere else in the world. Nowhere are intellectuals so eager, and feel so competent, to make history.

9:45 P.M. I went to bed at nine. The noise of the radio going full blast above me woke me up. I have to wait until ten before I can begin to clamor for silence. The man above me, a Negro longshoreman, may yield or not. If he has been drinking he won't pay attention. I hope for the best.

10:10. It's all quiet. I am going to bed.

November 11

Went down to the hall but wasn't dispatched. I called Lili and she, the boy, and I spent a pleasant morning in the park. We walked from 8th Avenue to the ocean, and then uphill to Cliff House, where we had an enormous breakfast. The boy began by being unusually affectionate. But as he wearied of the long walk he became moody.

I have begun to read Van der Post's *Dark Eye in Africa.* I do not as yet know what the book is about. The introduction is a tissue of existentialist double-talk. But as I leafed through the book it seemed I might find here something about the prehistory and history of Africa.

6:30 P.M. No. There is hardly any history. It is a discussion of African unrest in mystical terms. He objects to our "causalistic concept of life, our linear idea of a chain of cause and effect." He thinks that such an approach "to the mercurial soul and nature of man is dangerously limited." Yet to me there is a singular beauty in the lucid exposition of a linear chain of cause and effect. It can encompass intuitive insights and vague intimations, and need not be "dangerously limited."

His language is evocative and easy to listen to. He has a feeling of oneness not only with the black African and primitive man everywhere, but with man from the beginning of time.

November 12

Winter is here. I can see the dull, cold sky through the window. The clouds look frozen. It is cold in the room. Luckily, I have just bought a good comforter so that the bed is fairly warm.

I went down in the morning to pay union dues, and also bought a raincoat and a rubber hat—$16 for both. I did not like the owner of the store where I bought them. Had he given me the things for near to nothing I would still be afraid that I was being cheated.

It occurred to me that the most contagious manifestation of the soul is racial superiority. The feeling of white superiority penetrates even the least prejudiced mind. The Negro, too, cannot remain immune to the contagion. No one is so convinced of the utter worthlessness of the Negro as the Negro individual who made something of himself. I wonder how many people in Hitler's Europe were wholly free of a sense of superiority over the Jews.

November 13

Eight hours on the *Samadinda* at Pier 19. Loading lumber, mostly with a good bunch. The bay, seen from the dock, had surprising colors: leaf green of a most delicate shade along the bay bridge, and a band of pale purple on the Oakland side. The wires of the bridge have been painted with red lead, but they looked pure pink. Toward evening you could see the rain coming down, as a gray smear, across the bay.

I talked to several longshoremen, urging them to vote for Selden, who is running for treasurer of the union. Most said they would vote for him. One of the Slavonians snorted with disgust. I had to press him for his reasons. He did not want to antagonize me. I finally dragged it out of him: He was fed up with Selden's endless criticism of the union leadership. "Criticism is all right if you offer something better." He felt that criticism should be but as chili pepper added to a dish to make it hot. The offering of something better should be the dish. I agreed with him and promised to influence Selden in the right direction.

Just now it is raining outside. I have eaten a light supper of crackers, avocado, tuna, and a can of beer. I shall take a hot shower, and then sit down to read *Flamingo Feather,* a novel by Van der Post. This is the first novel I have touched in years.

November 14

Eight more hours on the *Samadinda.* I think I finally licked Section 11. It deals with the apparent fact that the birth of written literature in several ancient civilizations occurred during the first catastrophic breakdown of the social order.

I have been thinking about the curious fact that Little Eric behaves much better when he is alone with me than when other people are around. When he has an audience he shows off his power over me. I ought to qualify the statement: not when "other people are around" but when the family is around. Actually, when strangers are around, he clings to me. When with the family, he has allies against me.

November 15

Finished loading the *Samadinda*. Nine hours. It was bitingly cold and crystal clear. The bay kept changing its color from opaque blue to blue green, and the Oakland hills from blue to pink. Though the work was not hard, I began to feel weary and spent toward the evening.

During the day I scribbled a few pages dealing with Sections 12 and 13. Both sections, and perhaps one or two more, will deal with the nature of the creative impulse, and the manner in which the frustration of the unemployed scribe worked itself out in literary production. I am too tired just now to feel excited about the subject, but I feel I have finally got started.

I hope Selden gets elected or at least gets enough votes to make the runoff. He is poorly armed against disappointment. Failure will sour and twist him.

November 16

Eight and three-quarter hours on the *Hawaiian Merchant*. It was steady going all day. The pineapple discharged was of many marks, and the loads came out badly mixed. Luckily, I had Joe Monitz for a partner. We get along fine, and we both did our utmost. Time passed rapidly. I had no time to read or scribble. Nor did I have time to talk with anyone.

I made a good week's wages—about $110 take-home pay. I shall be off two days. I am homesick for the boy, but I shall not see him until Tuesday. Tomorrow I must rest and put my mind in order.

Selden did not get enough votes to make the runoff. He is probably terribly depressed, and I don't know whether I ought to try to cheer him up. I shall see how I feel about it tomorrow.

Finished *Flamingo Feather*—long-winded and unconvincing.

November 17

I took out from the library a book of essays by Georges Bernanos *(Last Essays)*. At last a genuine Frenchman. His directness and lucidity come as a surprise in these days of existentialist double-talk. One is no longer used to writing that says exactly what it means. Rivarol said that anything that's not lucid is not French. Most contemporary French writers are writing like Germans.

Finished Section 12. Very short. I know what Section 13 has to be.

9 P.M. Finished Section 13. It is all old stuff and I can't get excited. A peculiar dejection settled on me this afternoon. It may have something to do with my upset stomach. I am easily irritated. Going down Market Street in the afternoon I was fuming at the clumsy deception practiced by even the most reputable stores. It is an old trick which twenty years ago was confined to shady shopkeepers on skid row. Now it is practiced by all. The infuriating thing is that the trick works. An article marked $1.99 sticks in the mind as costing one dollar and a few cents. It is not in me to view things with alarm, yet this spread of deception affects me as if I were witnessing the spread of corruption and decay.

I went to the union meeting. There was no quorum and we disbanded early. Selden was at my side, yet I did not feel like talking with him. He is greatly disappointed by the elections, but what is there to discuss?

November 18

Just as there isn't a human society without speech so there isn't a human society without art. The origins of art are far more mysterious than the origins of writing.

After breakfast I went to Macy's to buy glasses for Lili. I bought six each of wine, brandy, and cocktail glasses for $11. Next time I shall get a tray.

I am intrigued by the fact that art is primordial, that its roots reach back to the earliest phases of humanization. It antedates toolmaking. Man used clay to mold figurines long before he made clay pots. When grubbing for necessities man is still an animal. He becomes uniquely human when he reaches out for the superfluous and extravagant.

November 19

Eight hours on the British ship *Colorado Star.* We discharged whiskey at a hectic pace. The sweating did me good, but my stomach is still upset. I return tomorrow to the same ship and more whiskey. During the day I kept thinking about Section 13. It should be possible to flesh it up and make of it a substantial thing with an impact. I get discouraged when I think what's ahead of me to finish the book. Yet, in all my writing I could never see farther than my nose—adding crumb to crumb.

November 20

Finished the job on the *Colorado Star.* Eight hours. During the noon hour I worked on Section 13. This kind of exercise acts like a tonic. Yet most of the time I am too weary for it.

How explain the primacy of painting, music, and dancing; the primacy of the non-utilitarian and the extravagant? Here are probably the roots of the uniqueness of man. Man's inventiveness is to be sought in his impracticalness and extravagance. All other forms of life are tremendously practical and serious. Man's creativeness has its source in his playfulness and his penchant for the superfluous. It is significant that to both children and artists luxuries are more necessary than necessities. We dare more, and are more inventive, when striving for superfluities than for necessities. Our utilitarian devices are mostly an application of insights and skills gained in the pursuit of the non-utilitarian.

November 21

Eight hours on the Dutch ship *Banggai* at Howard. The big Montenegrin whom I know as Negus was on the ship and we talked some. My impression is that he is becoming less radical, at least when talking with me. He has a passionate interest in history. I wonder whether he can read English fluently.

My partner was a Negro. While we were under the hook we saw two Malayan sailors painting the ship. They were typical labor fakers. My partner expatiated on the miserable wages of these sailors, and their wretched life whether on board ship or in their own country. I disagreed, saying that though poor they were not necessarily wretched. There was much joy in the simple life they lived in their native country. "No! No!" he said. "Over there you are either very rich or very poor. There is nothing in the middle."

At far intervals during the day I began to write Section 14. It deals with the relation between writer and rebel. The mood which starts the scribe writing is also the mood that breeds rebels. Both are prompted by the same impact, but their reactions are wholly different.

8:30 P.M. I have been working for over an hour on Section 14. I still can't understand why during the three weeks of vacation I was kept from working on these sections. The fact is that I have hardly ever taken time off to write. Writing with me must be an in-between thing. When it comes to rewriting it is different. But the first draft must be put together on the run. My chief difficulty is that I have not as yet a detailed table of contents for the book on the intellectuals. The outlines I have made are more suitable for a history than for a book of insights and speculations.

November 22

Eight hours on the *Hawaiian Packer* in Encinal. At noontime in the lunchroom the canteen man came over to talk with me. He asked whether I was interested in psychos. I said no, since normal people are more interesting and stimulating than the abnormal. Then he plunged into a weird discussion of the goings-on in the world since the beginning of time. There is something outside the world, he said, some sort of agency which at intervals infects our earth with a feverish agitation. Even the molecules of a piece of wood are affected by it. When such an agitating influence is on, history explodes. This is the reason why history is made in spurts.

It was only after half an hour of talk that I realized that his original question was whether I was interested in *cycles,* not psychos.

The gang I worked with today was all Negro. My partner was an excellent worker—conscientious and extremely willing. He has a swagger, and is not quick in anticipating things. But it was easy and pleasant to work with him. All day long Negroes from other gangs came visiting, and I overheard some of the talk. One elderly fellow eulogized the chiropractors, and particularly the one who was treating him. "Anyone say chiropractors are no good will get his ass whopped." His chiropractor had stuck an electric needle into him and had been treating him for arthritis, tonsilitis, and ulcers. "I never felt so good in forty years. He charges $250, and I am paying $25 a week. It's worth every penny."

November 23

I can't sit down to write. I can sit down to rewrite. I usually sit down to read or to copy, and then at intervals insert a sentence or so in the manuscript.

This morning I went down to the hall and wasn't dispatched. Only a few dockmen were called. I returned to my room, reworked

Section 14, then took a shower and went to see *The Seventh Seal.* Though the movie has no story, I found it wholly absorbing. The re-creation of the Middle Ages and the excellent acting were fascinating. Actually, when a moving picture deals with a remote era, the mere breathing of life into any common episode of that time is enough. A story might perhaps diminish the authenticity, since all stories are contemporary. The reactions and responses of individuals are timeless.

My stomach is still bothering me. This has been going on now for a week and I am beginning to suspect that some growth is blocking the alimentary canal. I have no pain, and I am not panicked. But I have the feeling that everything, including death, is possible.

November 24

Didn't feel like going to work. I spent most of the day shopping. A huge tiger for Eric, and a wooden tray for Lili. It cost about $25.

At noon I noticed the headlines about a terrific slump in the prices of stocks. I felt quite cheered. There is no doubt malice in this attitude, but my gloating had also a legitimate reason. Rising stock prices have often meant a rise in prices generally. A devaluation of wages and savings is a more general and grievous calamity than the busting of thousands of gamblers.

I wrote very little during the day. Section 15 will deal with scribes as sages and prophets, and Section 16 with scribes as schoolmasters. It will need vigorous writing to show that the scribe began to shape history when he lost power. Creativeness and moral fervor are phenomena of a stretched soul, and the stretching of the soul is brought about not by the possession of power, but by the insecurity of individual autonomy—by detaching the scribe from either church or state apparatus.

It goes without saying that the scribe does not relish his insecurity. He strives with all his might, whether he knows it or not, to create an order of things in which the scribes' usefulness is unequivocal—which is to say an order run and dominated by scribes.

November 25

11:30 A.M. Bought *Doctor Zhivago* at the Bonanza bookstore. The girl at the store seemed glad to see me. She gave me the only copy on hand, which she was apparently reading. The book is a Christmas present for Selden.

The stock market is still falling. No one seems panicked. It is a peculiarity of our time that crises simmer but do not come to boil.

8 P.M. Spent the afternoon with the boy. Put him to sleep, and later took him to the park. He was excellent company, and easy to handle. Once we met his mother at Petrini's he became aggressive. He senses disapproval before you utter a word. He either shouts, "Stop! Stop!" or begins to hit you.

I have been reading *Doctor Zhivago*. Not very exciting so far.

November 26

Eight hours on the Norwegian ship *I Gadi* at Pier 9. I felt in good shape. Though tired toward the end I was not irritable.

All through the day I was worked up by an article in the latest issue of the *Nation*. A would-be maker of history by the name of Birnbaum vents his irritation with the mass of people in the Western democracies. What riles him is that the common people "consume," seem to enjoy their private lives, and show no interest in "general political programs." Here is a mediocre mind throwing its weight around.

9 P.M. I am more tired than I had imagined. I am reading *Doctor Zhivago*—181 pages so far. Interesting but not soul-stirring.

November 27

6:30 P.M., Finished *Doctor Zhivago.* The book reads easily, never drags, and holds one's interest. It is only in the last hundred pages that one's heart becomes involved. It is not in a class with Dostoevsky and Tolstoi. Still, no other book gave me so poignant a picture of the criminal magnitude of the Russian Revolution. But Russia has recovered. The aftermath of the revolution has not been like the aftermath of the great calamities of the past, such as the Mongol invasion. One can decry nationalism and damn it as a monstrous perversion. Yet it gives immortality to the societies of the present. It is national pride that raised Germany from the ashes, and it was a chief factor in Russia's recovery from revolution and war.

November 28

Eight hours on the German ship *Saarland* at Pier 24. Last night I went to sleep at 8 P.M. and was up at 3 A.M. As a result I felt sleepy all day. The work though very steady was not too hard. I met a Russian longshoreman who has read the Russian edition of *Doctor Zhivago.* In the past whenever we came together we discussed Russian literature. His verdict on the Pasternak book: "It is a today book." He probably meant that it is not an immortal book. I told him that what I got out of the book was an impression of the Russian Revolution as an unprecedented crime: its murder of millions; its destruction of towns and villages; the unspeakable suffering it had inflicted on men, women, and children of all classes. He said this was true, but it was not new to him since he had experienced the revolution. The question is how many people in Russia share Pasternak's view of the revolution. One wonders whether the killings of forty years have exterminated the genes of moral courage and outrage. The indomitable spirits were killed off. Stalin's murder of the potent words of *freedom, justice, truth, honor* has left people without moral defenses and weapons.

10 P.M. Have been at the table fiddling around with notebooks for a couple of hours, and now, after a hot shower, I feel rested and almost contented. I shall get up at five tomorrow since I still have the job at Pier 24.

While taking the shower I have been thinking about Little Eric. He is extremely impatient of being ordered about. 1f you tell him that he must not do this or that he begins to hit you. Still and all, he is good company and I can spend hours with him without wearying. I see him usually once a week, on Tuesday afternoon; I put him to sleep, then wake him and we go for a walk. Though he resents bossing, he will yet remember the occasion which called it forth, and next time before we start out for our walk he will tell me: "I won't pick the wire," meaning that he won't pick a piece of wire out of the trash can as he had done the last time or "I won't eat the popcorn" but give it to the ducks as I had told him to do. Obviously, he has been turning things over in his mind during the week.

November 29

I have been reading a book on the Aztecs, *Burning Water* by Séjourné Laurette.

One gains the impression that the rise of cities and civilization is the result of a fusion of a sedentary, highly skilled population, and an invading population of warrior hunters who knew little of crafts. The substance of civilization was furnished by the conquered; the organization, particularly the evolvement of cities, was largely the work of the conquerors. It is conceivable that the priesthood was of the conquered population, and the fusion between conquered and conquerors was consummated by an alliance between the priestly and the warrior hierarchies.

I remember reading somewhere that in Sumerian the words for crafts and tools are non-Sumerian. The same might be true in the Greek language, in Sanskrit, and in other languages.

In Egypt, the skills and crafts came from the Delta, and the organization from the south, from upper Egypt. In Mesopotamia the situation was similar: the native dwellers of the lowlands, on the Persian gulf, had the skills and the Sumerians brought the organization. In Greece, the crafts came from the Pelasgians and the organization from the invading Achaeans and later the Dorians. The same was perhaps true of China and India. In Mexico the fusion was between the native Toltecs (a word which in Nahuatl means "master craftsmen") and the invading Aztec warriors.

What bothers me is the assumption that the momentous practical inventions and the crafts were developed in the relatively small Neolithic villages and settlements. Whoever heard of anything momentous being invented in a village?

November 30

Doctor Zhivago fills one with compassion for the Russian people. Has there ever been a happy period, a golden age, in Russian history? The presence of an obedient, longsuffering vast population can be a deadly peril to mankind.

My impression is that in the Western democracies just now people are weary of history. They view the future as a leech sucking the lifeblood of the present. Even the leaders are weary of history making. In Eastern Europe, too, people are hungry for the joys of the present, and see their leaders' preoccupation with history as a worship of Moloch.

December 1

A depressing, empty day. Eight hours on the *Kiska* at Pier 32. Petty grievances against helpless people filled my mind. Yet I cannot help myself.

December 2

It is fantastic how much of a feeling of well-being I can derive from performing duties. Today I took care of the laundry; mailed figs, dates, and money to Sara; paid dues and signed up in the hall; drew a hundred dollars from the bank for Lili. By the time I got through I was so much at peace with myself that I went and bought half a dozen roses for the room.

Recently I came across several instances where the term Americanization was used in connection with workingmen. When a workingman becomes Americanized you no longer can spot him on the street as a workingman. He begins to look and act like everyone else, and only by looking at his hands can you tell he is a workingman. In business, Americanization means a cut in red tape and probably also in supervisory personnel. There is also a blurring of the division between different kinds of business. The workingman benefits more from Americanization than any other segment of the population. The one who suffers most is, of course, the intellectual. Not only is the American attitude disdainful of the chattering, posturing intellectual, but by curtailing supervision it robs the intellectual of many opportunities for positions of prestige and power.

December 3

I have been reading Galbraith's *Journey to Poland and Jugoslavia.* On page 20 he describes the grandeur of a Polish church and the magnificence of the ritual and the music. Surely it is true, as Lecky said, that religion is the romance of the poor. What secular institution could offer day in, day out, such moving spectacles?

The poor had another romance—America. Here the humble might see their wildest daydreams come true.

Selden has become a diet faddist. How true is it that true believers have an affinity for diet cults? You attain immortality either by embracing an eternal cause or by living forever. Selden has always chewed his food methodically, so many times on one side, and so many on the other side. He never smoked. There is a link between faith and the mechanical. Fanatical faith turns people into predictable machines.

December 4

Eight hours on the German ship *Henriette Wilhelmine Schulte* at Pier 31. It was a very easy and pleasant day. We discharged sixty cars. Time went by fine.

Yesterday I found a telegram from the *New York Times Magazine* asking for an article (two thousand words) on the brotherhood of man. My feeling is that I could not write more than five hundred words, and it would be on how much easier it is to love humanity as a whole than to love one's neighbor.

Most of the day I felt in a particularly playful mood, and at one with the people around me. Have I missed much by spending my life with barely literate people? I need intellectual isolation to work out my ideas. I get my stimulation from both the world of books and the book of the world. I cannot see how living with educated, articulate people, skilled in argument, would have helped me develop my ideas.

December 5

Six hours on the *Dowa Maru* at Pier 23. We started 10 A.M. and finished 5 P.M. There was little to do—about 80 tons for two gangs.

During the day I tried to follow a train of thought started by the telegram from the *New York Times.* Are we likely to love our fellow men most if we consider them our brothers? Actually it is not a question of love but of tolerance—of putting up with people, and managing to be pleasant and benevolent. It seems to me that the attitude most fruitful of benevolence is the viewing of ourselves and others as strangers on this planet—as tourists (fellow travelers) on a journey. Tourists are usually brotherly with each other. In the latest *Reporter* there is an interview with Boris Pasternak in which he says that we are "guests of existence."

December 6

Eight and a half hours on a Grace Line ship at Pier 37. We discharged canned tuna from Peru. A busy but not a hard day. I did not touch a pencil all day.

I could stop working for the rest of the year, but I am afraid to do it. My plan is to work one more week, until the 15th, and then take it easy. I have on hand the following sums:

Cash	$103
Check	59
Check coming	100
Check for next week	100
	$362

If I layoff on the 15th I won't have any new money coming until the middle of January. This means that the money must last me for five weeks. This makes out $72 a week. Actually it will come to less since I have to pay rent, dues, and the boy's tuition at the nursery school. So it comes to $60 a week, which is not enough. I'll be spending money like water round Christmas. I must keep on working until December 21, take off ten days and go back to work January 2. This will give me $100 more.

December 7

I am reading Trotsky's *Diary in Exile.* A perpetual juvenile. He values seriousness and dedication above all virtues. An engineer, he says, can build a machine reluctantly, but you cannot write a poem reluctantly. It did not occur to him that you can invent a machine or write a fine poem playfully.

He is convinced that people cannot be decent unless they have a great idea which raises them "above personal misery, above weakness, above all kinds of perfidy and baseness," To a Trotsky, the mass of people who do the world's work without fuss and feathers are morally debased.

I wonder how many share my loathing for self-appointed soul engineers who see it as their sacred duty to operate on mankind with an ax.

December 8

Eight hours on the Dutch ship *Lombock* at Pier 19. A pleasant day, and since I am to be off two days I felt lighthearted.

During the day I had two afterthoughts which I like. The first connected with the relation between the playful and the utilitarian. I have harped on the primacy of the playful: that most utilitarian devices had their ancestry in playful practices; that the clay figurine preceded clay pot, and that the bow was a musical instrument before it became a weapon. Actually the relation is circular—the utilitarian may give rise to the playful. Playful pictures preceded utilitarian picture writing, but hieroglyphic writing often served an ornamental purpose. The same is true of the relation between ornaments and clothes: Ornaments preceded utilitarian clothes, but clothes often became ornamental.

The second afterthought concerns the relation between originality and borrowing. Our originality shows itself most strikingly not in what we wholly originate but in what we do with that which we borrow from others. If this be true it is obvious that second-rate writers or artists may stimulate our originality more than first-rate ones, since we borrow more readily from the former.

December 9

Spent the afternoon with the boy. We had a good time together. We went to Fisherman's Wharf and saw all the sights. He has an unlimited capacity for playing. Lili met us round six o'clock.

I am reading *Arabian Destiny* by Jacques Benoist-Méchin. The English translation was published this year, yet it is out of date. The simple fact is that the Arab world is following the Latin-American pattern. There is no fateful trend, no destiny, but endless, senseless convulsions. The literate segment of the Arabian population is reaching out for power. Every student sees himself as a potential prime minister or dictator. There are endless declamation, endless intrigues. No one wants to do a lick of work.

December 10

A Negro whore must have moved into the room underneath me. First night she did a gold-rush business which kept me awake until past midnight. Tonight, the moment I hear somebody knocking on her door I open the window and call out into the dark: "She don't live here any more!"

Living among people yet being alone is the most favorable condition for the creative flow. It is a condition found in a city but not in a village or a small town. Routine, lack of excitement, plus a modicum of boredom and disgust are other ingredients of the creative situation. Most of the time the creative impulse is a mild reaction against a mild, continuous irritation. Just so the oyster reacts with a pearl against the continuous irritation of a grain of sand lodged in its flesh.

Is commonness compatible with uncommon achievements? Does the creative person need a sense of uniqueness, a clearly marked separation from the common mass, in order to realize and exercise his talents? I snort any time I come across the statement that "all artists want fame, glory, immortality." My feeling is that once cultural achievements are considered as worthwhile and useful, and are as munificently rewarded, as achievements in business, technology, and politics, a mass civilization would be as culturally creative as an aristocratic civilization.

December 11

Eight hours on the *Santa Anita* at Pier 37. It was an easy, pleasant day and my mind was working. I can now see my way to write the article on brotherhood for the *New York Times*. I might push it through before the new year.

I am reading the memoirs of Tolstoi's sister-in-law. In 1869, on a trip away from Yasnaya Polyana, Tolstoi was suddenly seized by an overwhelming fear of death. What he feared most, she says, was to die on the road or in a strange house. He wanted to return as quickly as possible to his wife and children. The whole thing does not sound true. Is it really easier to die among relatives and loved ones? We die alone. Compare this with Montaigne's feeling when away from home: "I think I should rather die on horseback than in a bed; out of my own house and far from my own people. Let us live and be merry among our friends, but let us go and die among strangers. A man may find those, for his money, who will shift his pillow and rub his feet, and will trouble him no more than he would have them."

December 12

Eight hours on the *Santa Anita*. Steady grind. My partner was a good-natured Negro who did not watch the game, and I had to do more than my share. We talked about the Negro situation in the South. I talked. I blurted out that if the Negro is going to have genuine equality in the South he will have to fight and win it for himself. Anything given him by the Supreme Court or the Federal government will not mean much. No one can take away our disgrace. All we can expect from others is that they wish us well, pray for us, and at most give us money.

December 13

Four hours on the *Santa Anita*. Finished the job. In the afternoon I spent several hours with Lili and the boy shopping. The boy is a delight. Any day now he will be talking fluently.

The quality of a social order may be gauged by several criteria: by how effectively it realizes its human resources; by how well it maintains its social plant; and, above all, by the quality of its people—how self-respecting, benevolent, self-reliant, energetic, etc.

The elimination of the profit motive in Communist countries has not made people less greedy and selfish. The increased dependence of the many on the will and whim of the few has not made people more gentle, forbearing, and carefree. From all that I read it seems that the attitude of every-man-for-himself is more pronounced in a Communist than in a Capitalist society. The compact unity imposed from above has weakened the impulse toward mutual help and voluntary cooperation. Moreover, where failure may have fatal consequences, vying will not proceed in an atmosphere of good fellowship.

And yet, on the whole, there is less loneliness in a Communist than in a Capitalist society. People do not feel abandoned and forgotten in a regimented society. This perhaps keeps people from cutting loose from the Communist fatherland. The afterthought is that there is no loneliness in prison.

Again and again I come across the assertion that a society cannot grow and thrive without a culturally superior stratum which generates the impulses toward excellence and greatness. The axiomatic assumption is that, left to themselves, the common people will wallow in sloth or explode in anarchy. The happenings in this country refute this assertion. In the rest of the world at present there is evidence on every hand that the vigor and health of a society are determined by the quality of the common people rather than that of the cultural elite. It may even be true that the cultural elite performs best when society begins to decay. It was so in classical Greece, and it seems to be so in contemporary Britain. The sickness of Britain is not that its cultural elite does not write, compose, invent brilliantly but that the majority of the population are without the taste for strenuous effort. To produce a piece of machinery Britain needs twice as many men on the job as Sweden, and four times as many as the United States.

December 14

Eight hours on the Norwegian ship *Tancred* at Pier 28. A very pleasant day. Jack Lurie and the Montenegrin Negus were with me. I did a lot of talking. It is remarkable how urbane and gentle our idealists are in their treatment of brazen phonies like Nkrumah, Sukarno, Sékou Touré, and others. If an American soldier or businessman had displayed a fraction of such megalomania he would have been made the laughingstock of the world. But our intellectual establishment takes seriously the sheerest frauds in Asia and Africa. Nkrumah has a more than life-size statue of himself in front of his house (it cost about $200,000), and has his face on stamps and coins. Sékou Touré brags that he is going to institute forced labor, and revive the cutting off of an arm for theft, and you cannot hear even a murmur of outrage anywhere.

Now and then I wonder where my obsession with the intellectuals is going to lead me. If I could put together a small volume on the subject I would get it out of my system. But it does not seem I shall ever write such a book. I shall keep pecking at it the rest of my life, and sicken in the process.

December 17

The weakening of my memory frightens me. Unless I note a thing down it slips my mind completely. The effort to remember what I forgot results in actual pain.

I have been off two days and didn't do a thing. Still, I am beginning to feel better. The stomach functions, and I have slept well. Why not go on like this and see what happens?

Most of our self-appointed experts on foreign affairs are convinced that Americans are not intelligent enough to formulate a foreign policy. Both domestic and foreign intellectuals seem to have a vital need for the assumption that the people who built and run this country are stupid. They are not bothered by the mystery of how stupid Americans tamed and mastered a savage continent and made it a cornucopia of plenty. Nor are they bothered by the evidence from every part of the world that where intellectuals are in power everything, including the weather, ceases to perform as it should. The crops don't grow, or if they grow are not harvested. Nothing works smoothly and automatically.

December 18

Vanity manifests itself in overseriousness. To the vain, the trivialities of this world are of momentous importance. Everything that happens to a vain person is terribly important. Seen thus, vanity is the chief ingredient in the makeup of the true believer. It is equally clear how vital it is not to take oneself seriously.

December 21

It finally rains. I woke at midnight and the noise of the rain sounded like the chatter of a multitude. The unusual long stretch of summery weather at this time of the year had an unwholesome quality.

My days are darkened by the upset stomach. There is no pain, but it is clear that my innards no longer do their work. I have cut down on food. The effect on my mind is not noticeable. Worry does not interfere with composing. I am squeezing out, slowly and painfully, the article on brotherhood.

Quite often when I seem to lack the words to express an idea it is because I have not thought the idea through. When I know precisely what I want to say there is no difficulty saying it. The end of the article on brotherhood does not jell because I have not thought it out.

December 22

I cannot tell with certitude whether Little Eric imitates me or I him. It would be difficult to exaggerate the degree to which we are influenced by those we influence.

My attachment to the boy is as much a constant as there has ever been in my life. Yet at his birth there was no reason to assume that I could become attached to anyone. For I have been wholly alone for thirty-five years.

December 27

I have finished the article on the brotherhood of man for the *New York Times Magazine.* I don't know whether it is good. The train of thought is cohesive and original. I have copied it, and it should be typed and mailed next week.

I have been off now for about two weeks. My head works better. Chances are if I stay away from work I may push through the book on the intellectual. The trouble is that I don't like the book.

I am eating two meals a day: breakfast between 9 and 11, and supper between 6 and 7. Nothing in between. I sleep well, feel good, and could go on like this indefinitely.

What the finishing of the article demonstrates is that by hanging on I can make things grow—that this is the secret of composing. I need time and leisure to hang on.

December 28

It is back to work tomorrow. The material I have on the intellectual is not enough for a book. I could make of it a packed chapter in an entertaining small book on government by various human types. The book would have six chapters: rule by businessmen, intellectuals, priests, soldiers, aristocrats, common people.

I can sleep well in noisy places during daytime, but not at night. Noise at midnight is a monstrous aberration.

December 29

Didn't get dispatched—too many ahead of me. Nor is it likely that I shall work tomorrow. The waterfront looks empty.

To ibn-Khaldun, past and present were as alike as drops of water. It is perhaps true that everywhere up to the end of the eighteenth century individual life had an immemorial, static quality— despite the inventions and reforms. Even in this country people around 1800 lived the way people lived in 3000 B.C. What we know as the spirit of an age is a new thing. Throughout most of history there was an ageless spirit rather than the spirit of an age. In addition to the static quality of everyday life there has been the unchanging nature of the ruling class. History up to about 1800 was made largely by aristocracies. My hunch is that the spirit of an age is determined by the type of humanity that makes things happen.

The difference between the eighteenth, nineteenth, and twentieth centuries is only partly due to differences in technology. What counts most is the human type that dominates each of them—the eighteenth, aristocrats; the nineteenth, the middle class; and the twentieth, intellectuals. Had the machine age been initiated by aristocrats or intellectuals the nineteenth century would have had a different flavor and temper. The uniqueness of America is that here for the first time common people could and did make history.

December 30

Once man was tamed by the magic of priest and king, he stopped tinkering with and probing the world around him, and became a beggar—begging gods for good crops and good fortune. With the birth of the new Occident man resumed questioning the world and prying answers from it. He became a miracle maker and ceased to believe in miracles.

The typical intellectual cannot derive a sense of power from the manipulation of nature—from moving mountains and telling rivers whither to flow. He lusts to manipulate men. The dominant intelligentsia in Soviet Russia sets in motion vast projects to tame and master nature, yet uses these projects as a means for taming and regimenting men. The intellectual will not leave people alone.

December 31

Six hours on the German ship *Ditmar Koel* at Pier 15-17. We discharged cars. I was the only white man on the dock. It was not a bad bunch. The Negroes I know are probably the least introspective people in the world. There is so much in the outside world that they want, so many things they cannot have, that they simply cannot turn their gaze inward.

I return to the ship Friday.

January 2, 1959

Eight hours on the *Ditmar Koel.* A cold, empty day. Just now (6:30 P.M.) the heaviest fog in months has swallowed the world outside my window. I feel dejected. There is probably a link between my inability to get on with the book and the stomach trouble.

January 3

So long as we were ahead of everybody, America's banalities, vulgarities, and inanities could be accepted as perhaps an unavoidable byproduct. Since Sputnik our shortcomings and blemishes have become conspicuous and portentous. The need to catch up with Russia will have profound effects on our temper, and probably also on the social landscape. There is more talk now than ever before about the need for a national purpose. Our preoccupation with business, a high living standard, sport, etc., suddenly seems childish.

I am reading *Eastern Exposure* by M. L. Kalb, who spent the year 1956 in Moscow. The most absorbing part of the book is the record of conversations with educated Russians. The hunger for material things is greater among Russians than among us. The most important things in Russia are "money and connections." To hear them talk you would think that the young generation in Russia would barter its soul for a private, individual existence. Yet it is doubtful whether they could endure such an existence once they had it. They are not inured to the burden of free choice.

January 4

Eight hours on the *Java Mail* in Richmond Inner Harbor. Steady grind all day loading drums of DDT for India. My partner was a Negro. I have seen him on the docks before and the impression I had of him was of a labor faker. It turned out he was a fairly good worker, and a quiet, pleasant fellow. He looks sickly but did his share. We parted friends.

Marvin Kalb's book about Russia has set off several trains of thought. The great crimes of the twentieth century were committed not by money-grubbing capitalists but by dedicated idealists. Lenin, Stalin, and Hitler were contemptuous of money. The passage from the nineteenth to the twentieth century has been a passage from considerations of money to considerations of power. How naïve the cliché that money is the root of evil!

This terrible century has seen more attempts to realize ideals, dreams, and visions than ever before. We have seen the dissolution of illusions and the dimming of dreams and visions. Just as the nineteenth century saw a paling of the faith in God and in the kingdom of heaven, so the twentieth is seeing the loss of faith in man and in a heaven on earth. We have found out that when dreams come true they may turn into a nightmare.

January 7

Eight hours on the Dutch ship *Sarangan* at Pier 19. Loading lumber. An easy day, felt in high spirits most of the time.

The morning papers reported violent rioting in Leopoldville. For many years I had thought that the Belgians knew how to immunize the Congo against disaffection and revolt by preventing the development of mere intellectuals. Every educated native had to learn a craft or a trade and all the work in the mines, warehouses, factories, railroads, and even laboratories was done by Negroes. My theory was that the acquisition of skills, and abundant opportunities to exercise them, counteract frustration and disaffection. What I did not take into account is the role of example. The upheavals in neighboring countries would have released a social explosion even if the Congo had been an ideal country.

January 8

Six hours on the *Sarangan.* Last night I hardly slept because of the ruckus underneath. I have to rent a room to sleep in until I find a new apartment. The upset stomach and the inability to sleep have frayed my nerves. Perhaps it is all to the good: I shall be forced to get out of this cursed place.

Worse perhaps than the noise is the expectation of noise: the straining of the ears even when there is absolute quiet—so much so that I mistake the rumblings of my stomach for an approaching disturbance. It will be interesting to live for a week or so in two places at the same time.

January 10

The rented room in a hotel on Seventh Street was a bust. It was like moving from the frying pan into the fire. The earth-shaking noise of trucks and buses and the rattle of cars kept me awake.

Yesterday we worked eleven hours to finish the *Sarangan.* By the time I went to bed it was eleven o'clock. The noise downstairs woke me at twelve-thirty, and I was probably awake for half an hour. This means I had about five hours' sleep last night.

Today I worked eight hours on the *Tar Heel Mariner* at Pier 41. I return there tomorrow.

January 11

Nine hours on the *Tar Heel Mariner*. Steel all day. The work was easy but required constant attention. It made time fly.

I am reading Robert Guillain's *The Blue Ants*. He verifies beautifully my suggestion in *The True Believer* that mutual suspicion is the cornerstone of monolithic unity. Constant supervision, he says, is one of the keys of the system in Communist China. Everybody is supervised by everybody else; everybody knows that his neighbor is watching him. Reading the book you feel a stifling miasma wafted from Asia. Yet there are many in this world to whom the wind from the East brings hope.

January 12

Six and a half hours on the *Tar Heel Mariner* in Oakland. An easy day. I had a heated argument with several longshoremen about the trustworthiness of what Mikoyan and Khrushchev say. It is a waste of time to try to analyze a Russian statement. No one will remember a week from now what Khruschev said—not even he himself.

January 15

Five hours on a Dutch ship at Pier 23. My head was not busy with anything in particular, yet I felt as if I was mulling over something of utmost importance.

I find it significant that the recent riots in the Belgian Congo were led by one Joseph Kasavubu, a graduate of a Catholic seminary. The Belgian administration had taken great pains to prevent the coming into being of the merely educated. Education in the

Congo was linked intimately with the acquisition of practical skills. There were hardly any native journalists, lawyers, or university graduates. But the seminaries of the Catholic Church produced that which the colonial administration labored so hard to prevent.

January 16

Eight hours on the *Hakonesan Maru* at Pier 40. Hard work: nails, pipe fittings, and porcelain. I hope I haven't strained my guts. Most of the Negroes on the job were in a hilarious, abandoned mood. We had to do their work for them. It was payday, to be sure, but I have never seen such goings on. I must get some sleep tonight since I have to return to the same snip tomorrow.

January 17

Four hours. Finished *Hakonesan Maru*. I returned to my room at noon, cleaned up, and went to bed. Lili and the boy woke me up at four o'clock.

It is good that I live alone for I have a tendency to allow my inner discontent to color my attitude toward the people around me. I also seem to feel that a strong attachment to others narrows and stifles. Yet if I am not to sour and shrivel as I grow old I must see my attachment to Lili and the boy as a blessing.

January 18

Four hours on the *Wonorato* at Pier 19. I volunteered for the job. Working five days, since Thursday, I barely made $70 take-home pay.

I have been reading Herbert J. Muller's *The Loom of History*. The book gives a feeling of the passionate life which once animated the now desolate western coast of Asia Minor, and the striving for beauty, grandeur, knowledge, and power which stretched souls there for centuries. What concerns me is the fact that the trader—an essentially trivial human type—played a major role in the birth and growth of Ionian civilization. This civilization was the product of a fusion between the native population and fugitive immigrants from the Greek archipelago—the debris of communities shattered by the Dorian invasion. The significant point is that about the same time the coast of Syria and Palestine was also seized by immigrants—the Phoenicians and the Philistines—yet only in Ionia was there a cultural explosion.

January 20

Yesterday I spent nine hours with Sir Andrew Cohen and his wife, and the Iranian Consul, Rahenema, and his wife. Somebody in New York arranged the meeting. I talked too much and, made an ass of myself. Spinoza was right when he said that every time we open our mouths it is because of our vanity. It did not occur to me to listen and learn. Sir Andrew was governor of Uganda, and later British representative at the United Nations, Rahenema is the son of a Persian grandee, and spent much of his life in Paris. I ought to have asked questions about Africa, about Britain, about Persia. These two highly intelligent people had much to teach me. Instead, I talked ceaselessly.

Strangely, I felt elated when I returned to my room after nine hours of talking. It is only now that I see the ghastliness of the performance.

January 22

Yesterday we went to Stockton to see Cecily. The countryside looks neat at this time of the year. A fuzz of green covers hills and fields. The trees, though bare, glow with a silvery satin. Traffic was light, and we had a good time.

Today I went down to the new hall, near Fisherman's Wharf, but was not dispatched. How disturbing the change in routine due to the removal of the hall! Of course, in a few weeks the new routine will be firmly established and seem eternal.

My head is still buzzing with speculations about the role of the trader in history. My impression is that we know less about the origins of the trader than about the origins of other human types. The first traders were probably strangers—fugitives, exiles, and the like. Even in modern times trade in many parts of the world is the monopoly of strangers: Parsees in India, Chinese in Southeast Asia, Indians in East Africa, Syrians and Greeks in West Africa. For all we know, the trader is more ancient than the warrior. He certainly antedates the cultivator and the herdsman. The Ionian traders came to trade by way of piracy. The Phoenician traders practiced piracy whenever they could. The Philistines constituted a warrior aristocracy, and were not known as traders.

January 23

Eight hours on the British ship *Pacific Stronghold* at Pier 26. Whiskey. Hard work, but we were not rushed. I had for a partner big Charley, an old, slow man. I managed to read through the latest *Commentary*, but it did not strike a single spark off my mind. Hook's article about the Japanese, and a review of Stuart Hughes' latest books were up my alley, and should have stirred me up.

January 24

Did not get dispatched, and hurried back to my room before the rain got started. Now, at 9 A.M., I am at my table watching a gentle rain washing the world outside my window.

It strikes me as significant that the conditions which produced the first trader also produced the first individual. The emergence of the individual does not come as a result of social maturing, but usually in the wake of catastrophe. The first individual was an exile, a fugitive, an outcast, a straggler—someone cut off from the clan, tribe, or village. The incursion of strangers into a country will have one effect if the strangers come as individuals, and another if they come as a compact tribe or organized band. My hunch is that the Greek fugitives came to the Ionian coast as individuals, while the Phoenicians and the Philistines settled on the eastern coast of the Mediterranean as organized groups and not as a conglomerate of stragglers and fugitives.

What makes an explanation of the creative situation so difficult and uncertain is the role of example, of which in most cases we know nothing. The presence of a small group or even a single individual capable of setting the tone and of shaping attitudes may decide the nature of the resulting social, cultural, or economic pattern. I don't say that they who play such a shaping role have to be possessed of exceptional capacities and talent. They must have the knack of influencing others.

January 26

Eight hours on the Dutch ship *Duvendyk* at Pier 45A. A fairly easy job.

The renewed riots in the Belgian Congo make me wonder whether there can be a peaceful transition from colonialism to independence. Indeed, can any abrupt transition, any abrupt change, be peaceful? Apparently, drastic change, even under favorable conditions, is an explosive process.

How do the happenings in Africa affect the Negro in America? Were I a Negro the thing would weigh on me like a nightmare. Think of it: nowhere at any time has the Negro shown himself capable of creating and operating a free, viable society. What have 150 years of independence accomplished in Haiti? Where in the outside world is there a single Negro achievement, a single Negro personality, that the American Negro could be proud to identify himself with? Surely it should be the other way around: the twenty million Negroes in America should achieve something that would serve as a source of pride for Negroes everywhere.

January 27

Eight hours on the *Duvendyk*. Finished the job. My partner today was the Bohemian I know as "Reno." He is a man of some education, with a taste for words and a cutting sense of humor. His angular face (a combination of triangles) is very striking. When you talk with him you feel you are in the presence of a twisted mind. He is full of malice though ready to help his fellow men. We argued all day about Russia. He gloats over Russia's successes. As a Slav he derives pride from the achievements of his race.

I am reading Robert Brittain's *Rivers, Man and Myths*. On page 50 he describes the painting of the medicine man on a ledge in the "Trois Frères" cave, in the Pyrenees. It is the painting of a man disguised as an animal—a composite animal, embodying all the animal excellences the Paleolithic hunter so fervently worshiped. The eyes are of an owl, the ears of a wolf, the paws of a bear, the tail of a horse, and the genitalia of a wild cat. It occurred to me that the dragon, too, is a composite animal, embodying the excellence and powers of nature around us. On the other hand our devil is not a man disguised as a beast but a beast disguised as a man. What is the significance of this reversion? Perhaps the devil personifies not the nature that is around us but the animal nature, the dark primordial impulses, sealed in the subconscious cellars of our mind. Until we attain total humanization we are all, to a greater or lesser degree, devils—beasts masquerading as men.

January 28

To become and remain an outsider there is need for a degree of laziness and also of cowardice.

I took Little Eric out of school at noon. I have not done this for several weeks. I find him delightful. He still has no sense of numbers. He said he had three coats and showed two fingers.

On the way to supper it occurred to me that the juveniles who upset me so much were born in the early forties—after I came to San Francisco. They were babies only yesterday.

January 29

Eight hours on the German ship *Thorstein* at Pier 26. Something struck me today. Precisely at the moment when the world seems to leap into an unknown future there is an enormous eruption of the past. Not only do archaeologists uncover just now cities of unimagined antiquity (Jericho), but in the political field, too, the past is rising from the grave. In Eastern Europe we have a revival of the German-Slav conflict of A.D. 900-1200. In Palestine the dormant past of the Old Testament has come to life, and the stirrings of the Arab world echo the happenings of A.D. 600-1300.

Through the bus window on the way home I saw waiting on the sidewalk a Negro family—father, mother, and a daughter about ten years old. The girl had new shoes and a new coat, and she held father's and mother's hands. They presented a self-respecting ensemble totally free of the flash of juvenile delinquency one detects in most Negroes.

January 30

Eight hours on the *Thorstein*. Finished the job.

In my room I found a check for $300 from the *New York Times* for the article on brotherhood. I was not satisfied with the article when I mailed it; indeed, I didn't think they would take it. Reading it now I can see its merits. Still, the fact that it is better than I had thought it to be may affect my judgment in the future. It may stifle stirrings of justified misgivings.

January 31

Eight hours on the *Hawaiian Refiner* in Encinal. This is going to be a big money week. I am going back to the ship tomorrow and if I get a full day I shall have a take-home paycheck of $125 next Friday.

February 2

6 A.M. Yesterday I worked 7½ hours on the *Hawaiian Refiner*. I went straight from the job to Lili's house. Little Eric has chicken pox. He is covered with red blisters, but his vitality is not diminished in the least. She has had to keep him in the house since Friday, and as a result he is restless and full of mischief. I had a fine time at the Osbornes' until ten o'clock.

What strikes me again and again is the number of excellent people, people of gentle character and inner gracefulness, one meets on the waterfront. I spent some time on the last job with Ernie and Mac, two elderly fellows I have known slightly. I found myself thinking what fine persons the two are—generous, competent, and intelligent. I have watched them tackle jobs not only intelligently but with striking originality. And all the time they work as if at play.

February 3

A happy empty day spent with Lili and the boy. Lili is wholly herself, and the boy quite benevolent. He is recovering rapidly from the chicken pox. Whatever may come to pass later, the unadulterated pleasure of being with two human beings I love will leave a lasting imprint.

We went first to the De Young Museum to see the Denmark exhibition. There were tools, furniture, weapons and ornaments from the stone age to the present. Craftsmanship and a sense of beauty are evident from the earliest beginnings. The axes made of flint looked almost as if made of metal—so smooth and finished. All the bronze things are of the most pleasing design. There is not a trace of the nightmarish contortions and deformations one encounters in the civilizations of Africa, Asia, and pre-Columbian America. One is struck by the surprising effects achieved by straight lines. Surely the combined achievement of the people of the European peninsula from the Paleolithic to the present outweigh in quality and quantity the combined achievements of all civilizations past and present on this planet.

February 4

Seven and a half hours on the *Armistan Maru* at Pier 26. It was easy work and a good bunch, yet I came back to my room terribly weary. Only now after a cup of tea and some fruit am I beginning to feel human.

Early in the morning I wrote a fairly good paragraph on materialism and idealism. Poor countries must be idealistic, must use non-materialist incentives, to get ahead. A country must be affiuent enough before it can afford materialism.

There is a mystery: when I have a good reason to be satisfied with myself I find that people act warmly toward me and make much of me. It could be that justified satisfaction with myself affects my attitude toward others, makes me benevolent, hence their response. Still, it is possible that people can sense or even smell our inner situation.

February 5

I wonder what hope, self-respect, or perhaps even pride can do to a man's body. We are told that persons who wield great power usually have beautiful hands. Arthur Koestler in *The Lotus and the Robot* describes the Hindu leader Vinoba Bhave: His diet consisted of small cups of curds and molasses taken every three or four hours, a total of 1,100 calories a day. Yet his body was all muscle and sinew, his skin had a healthy glow, his gestures were vigorous, and on the march he could outpace any of the younger disciples.

February 6

Eight hours on the Chilean ship Almargo. A very easy day and quite pleasant. As I have noticed before, the men at this Chilean ship are more like intellectuals than sailors. Assembled together they give the impression of a university group. Our chief clerk told me that the second mate speaks English with an Oxford accent, and that all ratings have shelves of books in their cabins. Obviously the intellectuals in Chile are hard pressed for jobs befitting their status. The inadequate employment of intellectuals is a potent revolutionary factor. The Chinese sage Mo Ti declared twenty-five centuries ago that Chi and Chow lost their empire and their lives because they would not employ their scholars.

I am beginning to think that the activation of the masses—their readiness to work and strive—is a function of individual freedom. When the masses are left more or less to themselves, they turn to work as the most accessible means of proving their worth and usefulness. On the other hand, the ideal condition for the creativeness of the intellectual is apparently an aristocratic social order which appreciates his work and accords him rank and dignity. The intellectual does not want to be left alone, and this is perhaps the reason why he cannot leave others alone.

February 7

5:30 P.M. Finished the *Almargo.* Four hours. I am reading a symposium on new German history edited by Hans Kohn. Almost every attribute of the Germans contributed to the aberration which finally resulted in the Nazi monstrosity. The geographical position, the size, the diffusion of skills, and the capacity for work. Indeed, the German language itself was a factor. Somehow, the atmosphere of Germany was not favorable for maturity. In both rulers and ruled there was a chronic juvenility, with its exuberance, excesses, and inhumanity. Yet, to me, the seed of Hitler and National Socialism is to be found in the humiliation after the end of the First World War, and the devaluation of the mark. It needs an effort to imagine the disintegration of values which took place when the savings of a lifetime of hard work and self-denial became mere pieces of paper.

February 9

Ten hours on the *Loch Loyal* at Pier 45A. An easy but still tiresome job. Huge crates of plate glass. My partner was a willing but incompetent Negro. All day I had not a thought in my head. Early in the morning it somehow occurred to me that never in all my life have I prayed. I remembered Muhammad saying that three things had been especially dear to him in this world: women, pleasant odors, but the chief solace of his heart has been prayer.

February 10

The Chinese way of life which endured almost unchanged for millennia has been swept away by the Communists in a few years. Clearly, man is much more malleable than we think, particularly when the agent of change is pride. If a manipulator of souls can give people palpable pride they'll be putty in his hands. The communization of Eastern European countries is made difficult by the fact that it involves a diminution of national pride. In the satellite countries communization has meant submission to Russia. In China this does not hold true. If the spread of Communism in Asia will mean Chinification there will be resistance against it. With the aid of pride traditions are remade, and ways of life reformed.

One wonders how firmly rooted Western influence is in Asia and Africa. Certainly, all accounts indicate that the Chinese intellectuals did not find it hard to vomit all they have absorbed of the West's values and mores.

February 11

Seven hours on a Luckenbach ship at Pier 29. I worked with the bulkhead swampers on the breakup pile. It was steady going all day, yet the feeling at the end was one of pleasure. The pleasantness was due largely to the presence of Jack, the headup man—a highly competent and soft-spoken person. We did an enormous amount of work yet did not feel driven or frustrated. It made me realize again how a single individual can count in the development of a pattern of life. Yet we are told that it is circumstances and not men that make history. This is an age that saw the fateful role played by Lenin, Stalin, Hitler, Mao Tse-tung and others.

9:30 P.M. What is it that can grip my interest, concentrate my attention, and get my thoughts flowing? Judicious praise? Not quite. Verification of my theories and hunches? More so. Actually, the most durable and effective source of stimulation is a hefty body of manuscript wanting to grow.

I live in a society full of blemishes and deformities. But it is a society that gives every man elbow room to do the things near to his heart. In no other country is it so possible for a man of determination to go ahead, with whatever it is that he sets his heart on, without compromising his integrity. Of course, those who set their heart on acclaim and fortune must cater to other people's demands. But for those who want to be left alone to realize their capacities and talents this is an ideal country. It is incredible how easy it is in this country to cut oneself off from what one disapproves—from all vulgarity, mendacity, conformity, subservience, speciousness, and other corrupting influences and infections.

February 12

Eight hours on the Luckenbach ship. This was one of the smoothest and most enjoyable jobs. Today, time passed swiftly, and though I kept busy all the time I didn't have to strain myself. I had Macduff for a partner—a conscientious, slow-moving Negro. It was humorous to watch him complicate each job so that it became a difficult, serious affair. I thought to myself that, much of the time, this is the way religion makes life seem meaningful: by complicating.

7:45 P.M. I am reading Irving Babbitt's *The Masters of Modern French Criticism.* The essay on Renan confirmed my impression that no Anglo-Saxon can truly appreciate him. They cannot take him seriously. I wonder whether an essay on Renan written in the 1950s could be as patronizing. The Bolshevik and the Nazi revolutions have shown how profound and unerring were Renan's insights into the mind of the fanatic. The Babbitts, Santayanas, Arnolds, etc., were without forebodings of the future. Renan's grasp of the fanatical mentality, and the dovetailing of his interest in the past and the present, made him a good prophet. Like Dostoevsky, Renan becomes more timely with the passage of time. Yet who reads Renan at present? No one could convince an American that Renan's five volumes of the history of the people of Israel, written in the 1880s, are a greater aid to an understanding of the present than any number of volumes by outstanding political scientists, sociologists, psychiatrists, or any other experts. Renan's expertise was in the human condition, which is eternal.

February 13

Five hours on the Norwegian ship *Tancred* at Pier 26. A drunken Slavonian made life miserable for everybody. My irritation was intense, while the other members of the gang took the daylong nuisance in their stride. By quitting time I felt weary and dejected.

8 P.M. I am still reading Babbitt's book. A mediocre man, but I pick up a few things. I found a remarkable quotation from Brunetière: "The great error of the 19th century, in morality as well as in science and art, has been to mingle and confound man and nature without pausing to consider that in art as in science and morality he is a man only in so far as he distinguishes himself from nature, and makes himself an exception to it." He paraphrases him also as saying that man becomes good not by obeying but by resisting nature. I cannot think at this moment of a single book or even an essay that takes the opposition between man and nature the cornerstone of a train of thought. My hunch is that in human affairs all true opposites reflect in some degree the archetypical opposition between man and nature. God and man are on one side, the devil and nature on the other. Other true opposites: life and death, man and woman, civilization and barbarism, city and country. From this point of view the mechanical and the natural are not true opposites since both are opposed to that which is uniquely human. Moreover, nature is wholly mechanical and automated. To build something in the image of nature is to build a machine. I forgot to mention the chief true opposites: freedom and absolute power.

February 14

Nine hours on the *Turnadot.* One of the hardest days I have had in a long time. Seventeen hundred sacks of copra came out in 3½ hours. The rest of the day we spent sorting cargo. My partner was George Saraback, a Russian-Armenian with an unexcelled technique for labor faking. The sacks felt twice their weight, and the sorting was done in spite of the partner. Still, I felt good when the day was over. In 4½ days I managed to make almost $105 take-home pay.

9:15 P.M. Still reading Babbitt. I am repelled by his smugness. He has a position, connections, and "truths" which he will not offend by letting himself go. He lives in the midst of a herd of holy cows.

10:30 P.M. You can remember a feeling only when you have put it in words, or when it is connected in your mind with some sentence, no matter what. We remember readily what we see, hear, smell, or touch. But we cannot remember what we felt when we were humiliated or praised; when we hoped or despaired.

February 15

8 P.M. One is struck again and again by the innocence of British and American writers prior to the catastrophe of 1914. The French and the Russians had ominous forebodings of a great evil brooding behind the horizon, and strained their ears for the crack of doom. To the Anglo-Saxons such forebodings seemed symptoms of a chaotic mentality, if not of sheer charlatanism. The Germans (Heine, Nietzsche, Burckhardt) caught a whiff of approaching doom. Actually there is a considerable un-German element in the Germans I mentioned. Heine was a Jew, Nietzsche thought himself a Pole, and Burckhardt was a Swiss.

February 16

Four hours on a Norwegian ship at Pier 26. A beautiful job. We discharged fifteen cars and sixty-six drums of cyanide. No strain and no discord.

Another suggestive sentence from Babbitt's book (p. 181): "Science and Romanticism have cooperated during the last century in the dehumanization of man. What have science and romanticism in common? Obviously, a return to nature. Both science and romanticism are based on the equation *human nature = nature.*

February 17

Spent much of the day with Lili and the boy. He had his first bowel movement in the toilet this morning. So I bought him a present: a yellow raincoat and a cowboy hat. My feeling is that the boy is bringing himself up. It is he who decides what the next step should be. If he refuses to learn to read and write until he is twenty it will be so. No one around him has the inclination and the character to discipline him. I am full of forebodings.

8:45 P.M. I am reading *And the Bridge Is Love* by Alma Mahler Werfel. She is absurd, irrelevant, and sublime. Terribly vain, yes; but without the least trace of envy of those who create and achieve. She did not try to savor power by meddling and interfering with those who could produce. Most of the people in this book are musicians, novelists, poets, playwrights, painters— men of outstanding achievements. Yet there is a sickroom air about this world. They produced, but as people they were caricatures: pretentious, artificial, envious, malicious.

February 19

Yesterday I worked eight hours at Pier 32 on the *Hawaiian Packer*. My partner was an old, very pleasant Portuguese named Manuel. Despite the intermittent rain I felt joyful, and time fled. In the evening, as I finished eating supper, Selden rang the bell to tell me that his brother Bob has just arrived. I decided to go over to Lili's to see him. We sat drinking and talking until past midnight. Bob is wholly without defenses, and without a trace of self-assertion. He is intelligent, intuitive, and has an excellent memory. He is not normal. Most of the time he is lost in a haze. He drifts up and down the land, works at odd jobs, hardly talks to anyone, reads a lot (mostly avant-garde crap), and almost starves himself. Here is a case where a genuine belief in God would make a difference. He is obviously drifting to an unmarked grave in a godforsaken grave-yard. In lucid intervals he drifts back to San Francisco, but does not stay long. He sees most of the people around him as powerful and power-hungry. He equates power with arbitrariness. In his lucid moments he writes, fills whole notebooks, about absurd people who live underground, eat dirt, and invent question marks which serve as hooks to hang things on. He is obviously imitating the avant-garde stuff he reads. I have unlimited patience with him and the hours passed quickly.

Today he and I had breakfast at Mannings, and then walked to Fisherman's Wharf to see the new Longshoremen's Hall. The rest of the day I spent reading Alma Mahler's book. She venerated talent, and saw it as her task in life to ease the flow of creative energy. She exacted her due in pleasure, excitement, security, but not in self-aggrandizement.

A strange feature of the book is that the quotations from her diary are poor stuff.

February 20

Seven hours on a Japanese ship at Pier 23. An easy day. Rain and cold made it a dreary world.

In my room I found a letter from Christian Bey, a Norwegian intellectual I met several years ago. He has gone through the wringer recently—divorced his wife, and experienced some disappointment with his native Norway. He and a Polish sociologist by the name of Jan Serzelecki want to see me. I shall take them out to supper in the near future.

February 21

Seven hours on the same Japanese ship. I have been lucky this week with my fellow workers. Not a cross word or an unpleasant incident. It nourishes and enhances my benevolence toward people.

In the morning it occurred to me that the waterfront is the only place where I have felt at home. All my life, wherever I went, I felt an outsider. Here I have a strong feeling of belonging. One of the reasons is of course that I have tarried here long enough to take root. Yet it seems to me that I have felt at home here from the first month.

February 22

Nine hours on a Luckenbach ship at Pier 29. I am taking the place of a steady hook-on man. All day I had the bay before my eyes. The water was light green speckled with white caps. The hills beyond were wrapped in a powder-blue veil through which shimmered the mass of white houses. In the afternoon, over Treasure Island, there was a massing of dark gray and smoky white clouds. One could trace the roots of the white clouds in the gray mass, and the whole thing gave the feeling of a violent reaction out of which something wholly new might emerge.

8:15 P.M. The question of the readiness to work keeps tugging at my mind. My explanation of freedom as an energizer of the masses, and of individual separateness as an irritant which keeps people on the go, is not wholly satisfactory. These are valid causes, but not the main ones. There is, for instance, the fact that there is a greater readiness to work in a society with a high standard of living than in one with a low standard. We are more ready to strive and work for superfluities than for necessities. People who are clear-sighted, undeluded, and sober-minded will not go on working once their reasonable needs are satisfied. A society that refuses to strive for superfluities is likely to end up lacking in necessities. The readiness to work springs from trivial, questionable motives. I can remember Paul Henri Spaak saying after the end of the Second World War that to energize the Belgian workers for the stupendous effort of rebuilding and recovery he had to fill the shops and tease the people with all the "luxuries and vices" they had been accustomed to. Attlee, a better socialist but a lesser statesman, instituted at that time in Britain a policy of "socialist austerity." A vigorous society is a society made up of people who set their hearts on toys, and who would work harder for superfluities than for necessities. The self-righteous moralists decry such a society, yet it is well to keep in mind that both children and artists need luxuries more than they need necessities.

February 23

Eight hours on the *Old Colony* at Pier 46B. This was a time-and-a-half day, which gives me a good start for the week. In the back of my mind there is the question why I should go on trying to work four or five days a week. The real job before me is to write the book. But I have become a prisoner of my own routine. Though I have not deposited a penny of waterfront money during this year, I have only about $140 on hand. If I am to take out the Norwegian and the Polish sociologist for supper it will come to at least $30. On the first of the month I have a fixed expense of $62, which includes rent, dues, and the boy's tuition at the nursery. This means that I am earning only about $20 more than I ought to. I could work four instead of five days a week.

7:30 P.M. There is no particular reverence for leaders in the U.S. It is primarily women who generate such leader worship as there is in this country. This lack of worship goes hand in hand with the fact that in normal times the country does not need great leaders in order to function passably well. The ability to get along without an exceptional leader is a mark of social vigor. The same holds true of our ability to do the world's work with a minimum of supervision.

February 26

Eight and a half hours on the Norwegian ship *Besseggen* at Pier 7. It is a paper ship hauling newsprint from Canada for all the bay area newspapers. An easy and fairly pleasant day.

It is an established fact that most of the time on my days off I do not feel like writing anything. I am supposed to rest. It is conceivable that if I laid off long enough I would eventually come around to writing. But up to now all my writing has been done on the run.

8:15 P.M. The twentieth century has been more a century of leaders than the nineteenth. The concept of charisma strikes me as a throwback to the primitive. And who needs charismatic leaders? Intellectuals, women, and juveniles. The intellectuals' adoration of the power of words is a worship of magic. Women, too, are receptive to magic. The nineteenth century was a century of money worship, of the middle class, and of a preoccupation with the mastery of nature. The twentieth is a century of power worship, of the intellectuals, and of a preoccupation with the mastery of man. How innocent and naïve does the nineteenth century seem in retrospect!

My savage heart counsels violence and defiance against those who plot our destruction. Lately I find my reveries preoccupied with Khrushchev's shenanigans in Berlin. I cannot see any way out except resistance and retaliation. Those who counsel patience have on their side the fact that in our time crises simmer but do not boil over.

February 27

Four and a half hours on the *Besseggen.* Back in my room at noon.

My brevity is partly the result of a reluctance or inability to write. Delight in the act of writing breeds expansiveness. One shudders at the thought of the innumerable thick volumes which come into existence as the result of the sheer habit of writing. How many people with nothing to say keep writing so many pages a day in order that their body, particularly in old age, should perform its functions.

February 28

On getting up it seemed to me that I could not face a day's work. I stayed in, in bed. I shall try to work tomorrow.

Last night I went over to the Osbornes'. Little Eric was delightful in his reasonable conversation and his desire to please me.

This morning while eating breakfast at Mannings I noticed a well-dressed middle-aged man at a table. He was not eating, and he impressed me as someone who had particular reasons to be satisfied with himself—a well-groomed Englishman lost in pleasant reveries. What was my surprise when I saw him later walk over to a table and recover an abandoned newspaper. He had apparently been sitting there waiting for the owner to finish his breakfast and leave the paper.

Just now I am at my table copying sections of the new collections of thoughts. Drowsiness hovers around me, and the temptation to lie down is great. I resist it because a nap now means a sleepless night.

March 2

Eight hours on the *Powell River* at Pier 22. A very pleasant day on the dock. Production enormous: almost six hundred rolls of newsprint discharged by our gang, although we lost one and a half hours rigging and getting started.

Yesterday I was not dispatched. I spent four hours with Lili and the boy in the park and on the beach. I am particularly hungry for the boy these days. His passionate impatience of discipline disturbs me. Yet it moves me deeply to see him many days afterwards comply with something I have tried to impose upon him, and which at the time he resented. He needs conversation. I can see this from the questions he asks, and from his absorbed mien while listening.

I noticed several times lately that my memory is improving. I wonder whether the discarding of Tums had something to do with it. For years I used to suck on a Tums tablet the moment I felt heartburn coming on. I have not used Turns for about six weeks.

March 4

Five and a half hours on the *Matsonia* at Pier 35. Kolin's gang. Little to do, and a cheerful bunch.

As I was reading about Khrushchev's juvenile shenanigans this morning it struck me that there has been a process of juvenilization going on all over the world for decades. Almost all the leaders of the new or renovated countries have an element of juvenility or even juvenile delinquency in their make-up: Khrushchev, Castro, Sukarno, Nkrumah, Nasser, Sékou Touré—you name them. Arthur Koestler maintains that revolutionaries are perpetual juveniles—that there is something in them that keeps them from growing up. Now it is possible to see some family likeness between the adolescent who steps out of the warmth of the family into a cold world and knows not how to come to terms with it, and the revolutionary who cannot come to terms with the status quo. Then you look around you and you realize that the American go-getter who has no quarrel with the status quo is as much a juvenile as any revolutionary. Finally there is the juvenile character of most artists and writers. What quality can these diverse human types have in common? The answer that suggests itself is that all of them have a vivid awareness of the possibility of a new beginning; of a sudden, drastic, miraculous change. To a mature person drastic change is not only something unpleasant, but he denies its reality. He sees drastic change as a falling down on the face: when we get up we are back where we started plus bruises and dishevelment. The change that endures is that of growth—a change that proceeds quietly, and by degrees hardly to be perceived. To the juvenile mentality continuity and gradualness are synonymous with stagnation, while drastic change is a mark of dynamism, vigor, and freedom. To be fully alive is to feel that everything is possible.

March 5

It is good to be vividly aware that what seems impossible at one moment may seem easy at another. This drastic change in mood is perhaps a symptom of a weakened mechanism. But so long as the awareness is there the unhealthy fluctuation in confidence is endurable. I doubt whether anyone has worked out the rules which govern the flow of creative energy. What I know is that once I have waded into a subject and piled up a hefty body of manuscript, the thing wants to grow of its own accord.

March 6

Eight hours discharging frozen fish at Pier 17. Easy job, lousy partner. The chapter on freedom is evolving slowly. I wrote a few sentences between loads.

An old longshoreman I liked died on the job. He was a gentle human being and a passionate horseplayer. His wife died while his three children, a girl and two boys, were babies, and he brought them up himself. I have not seen them but heard about them—healthy and extremely well-behaved children. What's more, they are attached to each other and to their old father. He used to be a stonemason. His age—almost seventy.

March 7

Seven hours on the same ship. Finished the job. During the day I put together a few more paragraphs on freedom. If you judge a society by its books, paintings, music, science, etc., you are not likely to get excited about freedom. A regimented society run by a literate ruling class that rewards excellence and reverences talent might be an ideal milieu for cultural creativeness. Only the masses are energized by freedom. It is of interest that freedom is apparently vital for the readiness to work but not for the readiness to fight and die. De Tocqueville's magnificent sentence about freedom, that "it infuses throughout the body social an activity, a force and an energy which never exist without it and bring forth wonders," refers mainly to the performance of common folk. And yet it should be possible to create great works of the spirit in a totally free and equal society where he who writes books need not feel infinitely superior to he who sweeps the streets or prints and binds the books. The trouble is that some people do not want to be left alone; they feel oppressed when they are left alone.

March 8

Eight hours on the *Dona Alicia* at Pier 9. A very pleasant day. My partner was a Negro by the name of Flat Top. He is easy to work with. It seems to me that much of the day we talked about the problems of large families. Flat Top has five children, while the Negro winch driver Jimmy has seven. Both Flat Top and Jimmy are hard drinkers, although Flat Top is just now on the wagon.

Not a thought all day, and not a sentence.

March 11

Five and a half hours on the *Lurline*. I felt sleepy and tired. Through the haze of weariness I felt welling up within me a murderous rage against Khrushchev and the Russians. How can you talk with the swine? What do words mean to them? With us it holds true that even a lie tells some truth about the person who tells it. With the Russians it is not so: they lie on principle. It is significant that the dehumanization caused by Communism should be linked with the murder of words. It is perhaps a general rule that where human uniqueness is impaired words are emptied of meaning.

March 12

Eight hours of the *Oceania Maru* at Pier 41. Frenchie for a partner—an incurable drunk but of a pleasant disposition. He can't watch the game. Had an unpleasant beef with the Negro steward of the gang. The man talks and acts like a schoolmaster. I resented every word he said. He is going to put me "on the carpet." It will be an interesting experience.

For some reason my mind reverted to the problem of the readiness to work. I am itching to write a chapter on the subject. To me it is a miracle that 200 million people who are largely the descendants of rejects and dropouts from Europe should have created in this country the most important material power on the planet. I do not think that our engineers, scientists, and technologists are markedly superior to their kind elsewhere or that our natural resources are vaster or more accessible than those anywhere else. The unprecedented thing in America is what has happened to the masses. Never since the beginning of time have the masses had a chance to show what they could do on their own. It needed the discovery of a new world to give them the chance. It is the performance of the common people that made America what it is—the only new thing in the universe. I remember what Charlie Sorensen (*My Forty Years with Ford*) wrote about his visit to Leningrad in the 1920s. He found that in the higher field of engineering, like turbine building, the Russians were doing a pretty good job, but anything that had to be done by common people was in an awful mess. This was forty years ago, and it is still so today. Chances are it will be so forty years from now. Sorensen's conclusion was that we need not worry about Russia catching up with us so long as the common people are kept under the thumb of commissars. When you think of the marvels of food production achieved by Russian peasants on tiny plots of ground, and of the unmatched ingenuity displayed by Russian black-marketeers, you realize what a release of boundless energy would take place if the Russian people were told to come and get it the way this country told the millions of immigrants from Europe.

Soviet Russia knows how to foster the exceptional skills requisite for the manufacture of complex machinery and instruments, even the harnessing of the atom and the launching of Sputniks. But it seems helpless in anything which requires an automatic readiness on the part of the masses to work day in, day out.

Strangely enough, a similar situation seems to exist in democratic India. The director of industry and commerce in the Indian state of Andhra Pradesh was reported to have said that it is harder to provide people with shelter, clothing, and food than to launch a satellite. To a somewhat lesser degree this holds true even of Britain. There, too, the scientists and top technicians perform uncommonly well, while the mass of people see no reason to bestir themselves.

March 13

Eight hours on the Dutch ship *Friesland* at Pier 23. Hard work all day—asbestos from East Africa. We have to come back tomorrow to finish the ship.

Despite the hard work I do not feel too tired. Though not elated, I feel a certain lightness of heart, and I take delight in the neatness of my room. I had Emilio for a partner. He is an excellent worker, but he keeps up all day long a peculiar line of propaganda —propaganda for himself. It is not bragging, but he naturally assumes that every good thing that happens is due to his presence on the job. He is very good-natured, and goes out of his way to be helpful to others. His English is fantastically garbled. But when I try my Spanish on him he makes fun of the slightest mistake. I like him a lot.

I have on my table a bunch of grape hyacinths in a green vase. I have had it since Monday and it still looks fresh and beautiful. All the evening I have been conscious of the beauty of this combination of green and blue. Had I the ability I would have painted it again and again.

March 14

Seven and a half hours on the *Friesland.* Finished the job. About the hardest two days I have put in, in a long while. On the bus returning from work I had a sudden attack of compassion—for the young and the old, the successful and the failures. It seemed to me that in the whole world there was not one soul without its share of misery. I cannot connect the attack with anything that happened to me.

I am reading a small book by Klaus Mehnert on *Stalin versus Marx.* It is exciting reading despite my lack of interest in ideological subtleties. I cannot hate the dead—not even Stalin and Hitler. Yet my savage heart often rages with murderous fury against the living malefactors. My hunch is that the twentieth century will be a continuous hell to the end—one crisis after another—until all passions have burned themselves out.

March 16

6 A.M. Yesterday I worked on the Norwegian ship *Tudor* at Pier 26. Sacks again—this time copra. In the evening I went straight from the job to Lili's house. I had a fine time drinking, eating, and talking. We were all of us in a benevolent mood. On returning to my room I took a shower and fell immediately asleep. Just now I am at my table feeling rested.

There is not going to be a book on the intellectual. This is certain. Every article I have written during this decade seems to fit into a pattern. My subject is change: why it is so difficult in the Communist countries and in the new nations. The intellectual is trying to direct and master the process of change. If I manage to write a few more articles—on the readiness to work, freedom, the connection between technical modernization and social primitivization—I will have a book. Its title should be *Explosive Change.* [*]

A comprehensive theory of change should be applicable not only to the change from backwardness to modernity, but also to the change from boyhood to manhood, from poverty to affluence, from subjection to equality, and even to the menopause.

---

[*] Published in 1963 under the title *The Ordeal of Change.*

March 17

At noon I took the boy from the nursery school and traveled to the Hitchrack restaurant on the beach. I am beginning to realize that I cannot be impulsive with the boy. I must be deliberate and learn to impress him. I tried to be reserved, not show too much affection, and he behaved excellently.

Lili joined us at the restaurant. She had received a vile letter from a woman she had known all her life which reduced her to tears. Pious verbiage can be a camouflage for venom.

8:45 P.M. The readiness to work is still tugging at my mind. Pride undoubtedly plays a considerable role. It is a mark of modern man's desperate need for pride that he finds the weight of sin much lighter than the weight of weakness. It is disconcerting that despite its monstrous transgressions under Hitler, Germany seems yet to be the one European country with an unimpaired pride. Defeat in the Second World War has not blurred the awareness in most German minds that no nation by itself—however vast in territory, population, and resources—is Germany's match; that it needed the mobilization of the whole world to bring Germany to its knees. Thus the Germans alone among the Europeans are not oppressed by a vitiating sense of impotence, and it is their unimpaired pride that accounts for their astounding capacity for recovery.

March 18

Eight hours on the *Banggai* at Pier 19. I am having a run of bad luck. Everything I touch is hard work. Last week I had two days of asbestos, one day of copra, and one day tough sorting on the Japanese ship. Today I found myself working in the only hatch that had tapioca. I did not have anything to read so I made myself write.

Right now we ought to know all we can about the chemistry of pride. Pride—in a nation, a race, a religion, a party, or a leader—is a substitute for individual self-respect. In other words, pride is a vital necessity when we are in the antechamber of self-respect, and it matters not whether we are in the antechamber on the way in or on the way out. The present fierce craving for pride is indicative of the enormous difficulty experienced by people (particularly educated people) in maintaining their self-respect.

March 19

Eight hours on the *Banggai.* An easy day. My partner was a good-natured drunk, a Negro who has in him a will to work. The distance between the average and the good worker is greater among Negroes than among Whites. Progress consists in narrowing the distance between the average and the exception. We need biographies of the exceptionally good Negro workers on the waterfront. My partner came from a small town in Missouri. There were only a few Negroes, and he went to the one school. His mother was a nurse. He is coal-black.

I am too familiar with my ideas to savor their originality. The article on brotherhood for the *New York Times* was a mosaic of ideas I have lived with for a long time. I had great misgivings about the piece. The fact that the article made some impression on all sorts of people has revived my awareness of the originality of the ideas. If, then, intercourse with other people can be stimulating, it will be partly because it makes it possible for me to savor again the originality of my ideas. But for this you need people who will know an original idea when they see it.

March 20

6:30 P.M. Five and a half hours to finish the *Banggai.* On returning to my room I was seized by a fit of drowsiness which I could not resist. Now rested and bathed I am at my table itching to sort out the train of thought that has been trying to emerge for the past several days.

If, as seems to be true, my chief preoccupation is with change, then practically everything I have written should be connected with this theme. Mass movements, the true believer, the intellectual, the masses, freedom, America, the Occident, the antagonism between man and nature should all be facets and phases of the phenomenon of change. All the movements which convulsed the Occident for 150 years, all the human types that came to dominate the scene, all the views and doctrines and theories that found acceptance should be in one way or another connected with the inducement of human plasticity indispensable for survival in ceaselessly changing societies. I can see the dovetailing of nationalism, industrialization, militarism, revolution, the scientific view of man and his soul, the romantic return to nature, the proliferation of cartels and unions—I can see the dovetailing of all these into a vast unconscious effort to induce unbounded human plasticity. The originators of these movements, organizations, processes, methods, doctrines, views, and tendencies were often pulling in opposite directions; each had his own motives and aims, yet they all tended toward a common goal.

Put in a few simple words the idea has a strange impact: change has been the cause of revolution, of world wars, of Lenin and Hitler, of Marx, Nietzsche, Wagner, and Freud.

March 21

Terribly tired. Worked 8½ hours sorting cargo on Pier 29.

I was out of breath most of the day. The loads came out terribly mixed, and there was no end to the sorting. I straightened up only twice during the morning—at ten and at twelve. Still, during the day I tried to hang on to the train of thought I outlined last night.

Why was drastic change so rare until 1800? Obviously, as I have pointed out in *The True Believer,* those who are awed by their surroundings do not think of change, no matter how miserable their condition. The development of science in the seventeenth and eighteenth centuries generated an ever-mounting feeling of man's omnipotence among the educated. Tocqueville has described eloquently this exaggerated feeling of self-confidence which was coming to a head toward the end of the eighteenth century, and how, joined with this feeling, a universal thirst for change came unbidden to every mind.

March 22

Four hours discharging the *Hawaiian Packer* in Encinal. We worked 1-5 in the afternoon. Easy and pleasant. In the morning, while sitting in the hall, it occurred to me how almost all utopias when given a chance of realization develop a more or less regimented social order. Whether the ideal society patterns itself upon the family, church, school, or army it tends to approach the model of a prison. Thus the quest for individual freedom may figure as an escape from a realized ideal.

8:15 P.M. It seems strange that I should feel so good. I try to savor the feeling of well-being to the full, knowing that it won't last. My body is awakening from its long torpor.

March 23

No country is a good country for its juveniles. Like newly arrived immigrants the juveniles will adjust themselves to the status quo when they are given unlimited opportunities for successful action—for proving their manhood. There is a fascinating circular process involved. The strain of drastic change cracks the uppermost, mature layers of the mind and lays bare the less mature layers. Drastic change juvenilizes or even infantilizes. The infant is plastic. But the crucial point is that the juvenile will adjust himself to the new only when he is given abundant opportunities to prove his manhood. The explosions and convulsions which attend change are a sort of juvenile delinquency. Another way of putting it is that every drastic change recapitulates to some extent the change from boyhood to manhood.

March 25

Eight hours loading the *Hawaiian Merchant* in Encinal. An easy and very pleasant day, yet in the evening I feel terribly oppressed. There is no earthly reason why I should not enjoy life— live in a nice room, have fine clothes, build up an excellent library, and listen to all the good music there is. I must write for the simple reason that writing is vital for any feeling of well-being. I have no marked desire to see my name in print, and I certainly do not owe anything to anybody. I can go on thinking and writing at a steady pace, and let the resulting material take care of itself.

March 26

Was there ever a utopia which visualized a society free of planning, regulation, and supervision? Utopias are usually visualized by potential planners, organizers, directors, leaders. The envisioned new society is the ideal milieu for bureaucrats.

My feeling is that the age of utopia writing is over. We have lost our innocence and naïveté. We know something that most of the historians, sociologists and dreamers of the nineteenth century did not know. We know the end of the story.

March 27

Eight hours on the New Zealand ship *Waitenata* at Pier 26. It was lumber all day long—easy and pleasant. The depression of the spirit is gone and I am of good cheer.

It is remarkable that the intellectuals who cannot induce in the masses a readiness to work can induce a readiness to fight and die.

Who would have thought that intellectuals would excel in mustering armies, and be unsurpassed in readying backward populations for victory on the battlefield? The saying that the pen is mightier than the sword assumes a new meaning. The intellectuals are at their best in time of crisis—that is to say when there is need for magic.

The remarkable thing is that I do not think of myself as a grown person fit for responsibilities and great undertakings. It startles me to read of men aged fifty-seven—my age—who are presidents of companies or universities, or holding high political office, or even dying after a life full of achievement. Just now I read that Edward Gibbon died at fifty-seven.

March 28

Eight hours on the *Waitenata*. Finished the job.

I have been mulling over the opposites of freedom and power. If it be true that the human uniqueness of an aspiration or an achievement should be gauged by how much it accentuates the distinction between human affairs and nonhuman nature, then the aspiration toward freedom is the most human of all human manifestations. Freedom means freedom from forces and circumstances which would turn man into a thing, which would impose on man the passivity and predictability of matter. By this test, absolute power is the manifestation most inimical to human uniqueness. Absolute power wants to turn people into malleable clay.

The significant point is that people unfit for freedom who cannot do much with it—are hungry for power. The desire for freedom is an attribute of a "have" type of self. It says: leave me alone and I shall grow, learn, and realize my capacities. The desire for power is basically an attribute of a "have-not" type of self. If Hitler had had the talents and the temperament of a genuine artist, if

Stalin had had the capacity to become a first-rate theoretician, if Napoleon had had the makings of a great poet or philosopher—they would hardly have developed the all-consuming lust for absolute power.

Freedom gives us a chance to realize our human and individual uniqueness. Absolute power can also bestow uniqueness: to have absolute power is to have the power to reduce all the people around us to puppets, robots, toys, or animals, and be the only man in sight. Absolute power achieves uniqueness by dehumanizing others.

To sum up: Those who lack the capacity to achieve much in an atmosphere of freedom will clamor for power.

March 30

Yesterday I worked eight hours on the *Korean Bear* in Encinal. It was perhaps the first time I have worked on an Easter Sunday.

Early in the morning while waiting for the No. 19 bus I watched a longshoreman, incoherent with drink, mumble curses on the New York Jews, and brag that he was a Roman Catholic. At first it seemed to me incongruous that one should curse Jews on a day dedicated to a Palestinian Jew. Then I remembered that in Europe Easter used to be a time of danger for the Jews—the time for ritual-murder accusations.

In the evening I went straight from the job to Lili's, and spent several happy hours. What can there be better after a hard day than feasting with people one loves.

Today I cleaned house, cashed a check, and fiddled around reading and scribbling.

March 31

A beautiful day. In the morning I had an unusual feeling of well-being. I don't know what caused it. After breakfast I went around shopping for flowers but I didn't find anything to satisfy me. In my room I copied out several sections (mainly on freedom) and read Alexander Campbell's *The Heart of India.* Can a country so poor afford freedom? And are not the strains and tensions of freedom too much for a new country not oversupplied with technical, social, and political skills? To me it is axiomatic that a nation has to be affluent enough before it can afford freedom, and vigorous enough to stand up under the ceaseless tug of willful parties and free individuals. Above all, to stay free, a society needs skills so that its apparatus of everyday life functions smoothly.

April 1

Eight hours on the German ship *Birkenau* at Pier 28. An easy job, but I strained my back. Last night the union meeting went on until 11 P.M. I didn't fall asleep until past midnight, and I was up at 4:30 A.M. The result is that I am not feeling well. In addition to the pain in the back I seem to have a touch of the flu.

7:30 P.M. The problem of change is getting mixed up in my mind with the problem of man and nature. The human plasticity required by drastic change involves some dehumanization. In a sense, to become plastic man must become matter—malleable clay. Thus drastic change, even when it is a leap forward, results in primitivization, in a return to nature. And since absolute power tends to turn people into matter, you can see how the absolute despot fits into the picture of change.

One thing is certain: absolute power turns its possessor not into a God but an anti-God. For God turned clay into men, while the absolute despot turns men into clay.

April 3

The kink in my back is getting worse. I went down to the hall this morning but didn't answer my call. I took the bus from the hall to the ferry building to collect my check. By chance I bumped into a fellow I have known all the years on the waterfront yet never knew his name. He seemed very voluble. He pointed to his bulging stomach and said: "I can't climb the ladders with this, so I am working cars." He had a paper bag in his hand and told me that while eating breakfast he got into an argument with a Negro longshoreman, and in his excitement walked out of the restaurant without his lunch. When he later returned, his lunch was still there—no one had swiped it. For some reason he shifted the conversation to the union button on his cap. He said: "Where I live this button gets you in trouble. They think you are a Commie." I asked him where he lived and he said the Mission District. I told him I had a button on my cap all the time, and never worried what people think. I said: "If I kept worrying what people think about me I would wind up in a nuthouse." He took my breath away when he answered: "That's just where I have been. My sister called the wagon and they took me to Napa. I have been out only three weeks." I know that he had been working steady for several years. He always struck me as intelligent, good-natured, and quiet. Perhaps in the case of innately sensitive people the monotony of a workingman's life builds up a strain. By his look you would think that he would be at home where people argued passionately about ideas.

April 4

The first thing I thought of this morning was something I had seen at Lili's on Easter Sunday. She had put a tiny cloth rabbit in a dish of colored eggs and placed it on a blue tablecloth.

It is perhaps true that every man has a crucial decade. Mine was the Hitler decade. It colors my thinking, and shapes my attitude towards events. I can never forget that one of the most-gifted and best-educated nations in the world, of its own free will, surrendered its fate into the hands of a maniac. It did so not to gain freedom and affluence but for pride. Hitler was going to make Germany the most powerful nation in the world. The educated—professors, students, scientists, technicians, and men of the professions—served Hitler with as much devotion as did the ignorant and the simple.

Of course, few nations have known the defeat and humiliation experienced by the Germans after the First World War, and the soul-wrecking inflation. Who knows how we would act if we were defeated and humiliated?

April 5

I am beginning to believe that human uniqueness can unfold and endure only in an environment of stability and continuity. The incessant, drastic changes in all departments of life characteristic of modern society are hostile to human nature. It was probably inevitable that when change was beginning to gain momentum in the second half of the nineteenth century there was also set in motion a process of dehumanization.

What puzzles me is the passionate, blind effort by scientists, psychologists, historians, economists, businessmen, industrialists, revolutionaries, military men to hack away at man's uniqueness—to demonstrate that there is no basic difference between man and the rest of creation. It is a blind, concerted effort to downgrade man, and it goes hand in hand with an unprecedented increase of man's power over nature. Fantastic!

April 6

I am getting used to leisure. It is now five days since I worked last, I have not written much, yet I feel I am making some progress. I am free of restlessness and fear.

I have never taken time off to write. Yet the fact remains that the crucial advances in writing *The True Believer* occurred during the strikes in 1946 and 1948—three months each. The strained back may give me a couple of weeks of leisure.

10 P.M. What puzzles me is the enormous dovetailing between the participants in the historic process. Take for instance the lustful dovetailing between the manipulators and the manipulated. The absolute despot lusts to dehumanize—to turn people into things—while the weak, weary of the strain of human uniqueness, long to drop the burden of free choice. All the metaphysical double-talk about the *Zeitgeist,* world spirit, historic necessity, super-individual tendencies and the like cluster around this puzzle. I would love to spend the rest of my life playing with this puzzle.

There is such a thing as fashion in thinking. There was something in the air that both Darwin and Marx and others picked up when they elaborated their theories. The integration of man with nonhuman nature which preoccupied scientists, philosophers and writers in the nineteenth century—the romantics and the realists, the idealists and the cynics—had perhaps a common origin, and I have to find it. To say that the onset of the industrial revolution created a demand for a new type of man, malleable and mechanized, does not explain anything. Darwin and Freud had nothing to do with the industrial revolution, and the romantics were violently against it. The industrialists wanted money, the politicians power, the scientists searched for regularities. Each one of the actors wanted something different, yet they all labored at the same task.

April 7

It is raining again. The alternation of sun and rain makes things grow. We ought to go out to the country.

I notice that I am shying away from any reading material that is complex and difficult. To some degree this has been my habit through the years, but it is more so now. Histories, biographies, travel books, short treatises on any subject I read through. Others I taste and put aside.

4:30 P.M. Concerning the masses: They had only one chance to show what they could do on their own. But this demonstration took place on a virgin continent rich in natural resources. It was an exceptional environment which allowed the masses to squander, fumble, and fail without fatal consequences. Could the masses achieve aught on their own under difficult conditions?

April 8

Eight hours on the *Lurline.* Had Red for a partner—an exceptionally fine fellow, and it is surprising that it is the first time we have worked together.

My back is not quite well as yet. It might be a chronic thing. It is surprising that such a prospect does not panic me. Anything which puts me out of action might help my writing.

The sky over the bay is painted daily by a wonderfully gifted and sensitive abstract painter. His blues, grays, whites, blacks, and golds are breathtaking. He just smears on the paint and it always makes sense. Surely, the painters of the bay area should be of his school.

April 9

Six and a half hours on the *Lurline.* A very easy day.

I am rereading Jaspers' *Origin and Goal of History.* He is blind to trivial motives and causes. Something momentous, he is sure, started the axial period. To suggest that unemployed scribes set the whole thing in motion would be to blaspheme. The more or less sudden breakdown of the bureaucratic apparatus in many countries in the early part of the first millennium B.C. brought into being the unattached scribe—a scribe without status and identity. Amos, Hesiod, Confucius, Zoroaster were probably unemployed scribes. Jaspers also fails to recognize that the inception of the axial period marks also the birth of written literature in Palestine, Greece, Persia, and China.

April 10

I went down to the hall but was not dispatched. I shall take a nap and then go down to the library.

2:30 P.M. The scribe's role in ancient Egypt and Mesopotamia was not unlike that of a lawyer in present-day America. He was a multipurpose human type. He could fit into any field of human endeavor—economic, political, diplomatic, military, religious, and so on. The American lawyer is a potential recruit for corporations, universities, government, unions, banks and whatnot.

In every society there is a multipurpose type. In America it is the lawyer, in Russia the commissar, in Britain the politician, in France the writer, in Germany the professor, in Japan the Samurai.

April 11

Not dispatched. A letter from Norman Jacobson. He is going to give a series of seminars on mass democracy and the creative individual. From his outline it is obvious that he will deal mainly with creativeness in science. He wants me to give one of the seminars: I should describe the manner in which I first stumbled into thinking and writing. It will choke me to repeat the oft-told tale. However, I am interested in the creative potentialities of common people, and in the creative process in general, and should have enough ideas to play with for an hour or so.

Lili and the boy came about four o'clock. He is wonderfully alert, and his mind works much faster than his capacity for speech. He wants to ask all sorts of questions but has not enough words. Lili looked beautiful. We had a good time.

April 12

Ten hours on the *Golden Gate* at Pier 37. It was a long but not unpleasant day. My back seems to have straightened out.

How I rage against Khrushchev in my reveries. It is almost as it was in the 1930s when I raged against Hitler. Does my savage heart need an enemy to vent its fury on? And I can't separate Russia from Khrushchev. Russia: founded on a cesspool of bondage and gore. Whatever is built on this foundation is soon impregnated with an ancient stench, and made leprous with the ancient rot. Westernization means here cleaning up—a hopeless task. Culture: An interaction between the exhalations from the dark depths, and elements introduced from the Occident. There is a crackling and hissing, and a giving off of varicolored flashes and of fabulous odors and perfumes.

Martin Luther found that the rage against his enemies helped him to pray well. I ought to drain my rage against Khrushchev into thinking and writing.

April 14

I do not want to feel that I know best. I hope that other people—many of them—know better. For the counsel of my heart is often savage. And what do I really know about this country? I am without instinctive tolerance. The fact that I have not been to grammar school disqualifies me as a prompter of genuinely democratic behavior. When others counsel patience, forbearance, and kindness I ought to keep my mouth shut.

April 15

Eight hours on the *Keito Maru*. A surprisingly easy day, yet in the evening I felt dejected. It is so easy to be dissatisfied with myself. The least transgression weighs on me. To preserve my sense of well-being I must lean backward in my dealings with others. A sensitive conscience is probably a symptom of old age. I must be scrupulously decent not in order to feel noble but to feel well.

The lack of enterprise and venturesomeness in the British business world is not easy to explain. High taxes and excessive red tape are not the reason. From my talks with the mates on Swedish ships I gather that taxes and red tape are as high and excessive in Sweden, if not more so. Yet businessmen in Sweden are alert and on the go, and the rate of growth of the Swedish economy is satisfactory. Actually the fact that net profits remain moderate, no matter what, should promote risk taking. You need not worry about the profits. It is not true that people will exert themselves in business only for money. There are other prizes—power, fame, adventure, and sheer achievement. For a game-playing nation like the British, business played as a game should not seem outlandish. What we have, then, in Britain is a lack of exuberance and inner pressure. Do the old in Britain hang on longer to positions of power? Yet in Japan, too, the old are not discarded. Many of the Japanese tycoons look ancient. My hunch is that the prevailing ideal of the gentlemanly squire makes for leisureliness, under-statement and gracious living. Go-getting is vulgar. The British have not won many trophies in sports. The old Samurai tycoons transact business as if they were going to war.

April 16

Nine hours on the *C. E. Dant* at Pier 17. A weary day. Had Skeets for a partner—a poor worker with a bleating voice.

At intervals I peeked into an English translation of the *Lun Yü.* The aphorisms do not seem brilliant, yet you want to reread them. Perhaps it is because of the vagueness of some of the terms, the strangeness of the setting, and even the modernity of some of the sayings. "It is hard to find a man who will study for three years without thinking of a post in government." This is true even now in Asia, Africa, and Latin America. "To remain unconcerned though others do now know of us—that is to be a great man."

April 17

Eight hours on the *C. E. Dant.* Finished the job. Had a new partner, a Negro, very conscientious and nice to be with.

Something I read in the *Manchester Guardian Weekly* started me thinking about the attitude of the masses toward the intellectuals. There is no doubt that to most Portuguese and Italian longshoremen a schoolmaster is an important person, almost as much a dignity as the priest. But through most of history the common people resented the educated as exploiters and oppressors. Rabbi Akiba, who started life as a roustabout, recalled how he used to cry out: "Give me one of the learned and I shall bite him like a jackass." During the peasant uprisings the clerks were given short shrift by the mobs. When in the fourteenth century the mob burned the charters and manuscripts of the University of Cambridge an old hag tossed the ashes into the wind crying: "Away with the learning of the clerks, away with it."

April 18

Eight hours on a Dutch ship at Pier 19. Somehow. I didn't notice the name. We are ordered back for Monday, but I am going down to the hall tomorrow to get a time-and-a-half Sunday job. I feel like working.

It was an easy, pleasant day, and now at 7 P.M. I am without a trace of weariness. While taking a shower I thought confidently about the book on change. It will have chapters on the different kinds of change: peasants into mechanics; boys into men; slaves into free men; shopkeepers into warriors (Israel) and vice versa (Japan); and several others.

The transformation of peasants into industrial workers involves a leap from the Neolithic Age into the twentieth century. Everywhere you look at present you see nations trying to leap. In some instances the transformation runs smoothly while in others it is accompanied by social upheavals and explosions. It is not too farfetched to assume that the convulsions and tensions of the Occident during the last hundred years were to some extent a by-product of the uprooting of millions of peasants and their transference to city and factory. Perhaps the chief purpose of a Communist revolution is to separate the peasant from the land and boot him into the factory. Enclosure did it in Britain. Emigration to America was probably the least explosive instance of the transformation of peasants into mechanics. Something similar is just now taking place in Europe, where Italian and Spanish peasants migrate to Germany and France and there undergo almost painlessly the transformation into industrial workers. Apparently, the leap from the Neolithic into the industrial age is helped when there is an actual leap from one country to another. Stalin hurled the peasants of the Ukraine to the factories of Siberia. I wonder whether a leap from one faith to another could be equally helpful.

April 19

Six hours on the *Hakonesan Maru* at Pier 26. A very easy day. My partner, a fellow by the name of Palmer, is unusually quiet, yet today with a little prompting he exhibited remarkable descriptive powers. He described how he has organized getting out of bed, going to the toilet, washing, dressing, and cooking breakfast into a sort of assembly line with not a single lost motion. It was hilarious.

After work I went directly to Lili's, where I spent several happy hours eating, drinking, and talking. It is not an unhappy household despite the friction between the parents. Lili and Little Eric are so overflowing with vitality that there is no likelihood of prolonged sullenness.

April 20

Back to Pier 19 to finish the ship we started Saturday. It is actually not a Dutch but a Norwegian ship—the *Hoegh Silverstream*. An easy day, but the stretch of six days' work is beginning to tell. I am very tired.

In the book on change, the introductory chapter will outline the general theory, and the succeeding chapters will deal with the different instances of change. I have to remind myself that I have not the temperament of a scholar. I am not going to pile up carefully documented facts. If I can't swing out with theories, hunches, and guesses I am lost.

Afterthought: the chapter which outlines the general theory should come at the end.

April 21

The fact that I have read a lot and that I think and write has never generated in me the conviction that I could teach and guide others. Even in a union meeting of unlearned longshoremen it has never occurred to me that I could tell them what to do. This reluctance to teach and guide is the result not of a lack of confidence in myself but rather of a confidence in the competence of the run-of-the-mill American.

The important point is that the lack of the conviction that I have the ability and the right to teach others marks me as a non-intellectual. For the intellectual is above all a teacher, and considers it his God-given right to tell the ignorant majority what to do. To ignore this teacher complex is to ignore the intellectual's central characteristic, and miss the key to his aspirations and grievances. I am sure that the passion to teach has been a crucial factor in the rise of the revolutionary movements of our time. In most cases when a revolutionary takes over a country he turns it into a vast schoolroom with a population of cowed, captive pupils cringing at his feet. When he speaks the whole country listens.

April 23

Eight hours palletizing short four-by-fours at Pier 48B. The easiest, steadiest, and most wearisome job I have ever known. Time flew, but the leaden monotony was frightening. There was no pause to sit down or catch one's breath. I refused to return tomorrow.

I have been feeling quite empty since Sunday night. Tired and empty. It is peculiar that in the present mood I find most of what I read trite and wearisome.

It is more than two days since I saw Little Eric, but he is still with me. He has had almost from birth the capacity to impregnate me with his presence.

April 24

5 A.M. Karl Jaspers' grandiloquence moves me: "At the termination of history in the existing sense we are witnessing the radical metamorphosis of humanity itself." Or "Our age is of the most incisive significance. It requires the whole history of mankind to furnish us with standards by which to measure the meaning of what is happening at the present time." Does not mean much, yet

for a moment you feel as if he had given you a glimpse of the awesome spectacle that is unfolding in the whole of the world at this moment. There is a stirring of depths and a jostling of nations all over the earth.

And yet what a shabby, crummy, vain, and posturing lot are the men who engineer and preside over this spectacle.

The meaning of technology, he says, "is freedom in relation to nature. Its purpose is to liberate man from animal imprisonment in nature, with its wants, its menace, and its bondage."

4 P.M. Six hours sorting cargo at Pier 34. Steady grind but not unpleasant. The weariness at the end of the day is still here.

April 25

The first rain in a long while. Worked eight hours on the *Ola Colony* at Pier 40—the easiest day I can remember. Our hatch had nothing but vans.

On returning to my room it occurred to me that the title of the book on change should be *Change and Fanaticism.* It would underline the role of fervor, faith, enthusiasm, true believers, and mass movements in the process of change.

As I watch the rain-washed city spread outside my window I have a feeling that the world is again normal—back on the rails. There has been a leprous quality to the prolonged sunniness of the winter. The premature summer seemed one more symptom of a universe out of joint.

April 26

8:30 P.M. Eight hours on the *Ocean Joyce* at 14th Street. Steady grind, loading canned goods. A good bunch. I did not feel overly tired at the end of the day and looked forward to a happy evening at Lili's. However, things turned out dismally. I found there a woman with a big nose, big mouth, and a torrent of stale intellectual clichés. A regular horror. Instead of fending her off by keeping my mouth shut or by concentrating my attention on Lili, who was working in the kitchen, I stupidly got into an unpleasant argument. I was vehement and patronizing—sounded like a regular, superior intellectual. Now back in my room I feel tired and dejected.

April 27

9 P.M. I am reading *The Privilege Was Mine* by Zinaida Shakovskoi. She comes from a Russian aristocratic family (a princess), was brought up in France, and married a Frenchman. She visited Moscow in 1957. Her writing is delightful—lucid, precise, intelligent. To be civilized is perhaps to rise above passion; to be able to observe and report without giving way to anger or enthusiasm, and let the reader react as he will. Her book crystallized in my mind something I have known for a long time. The change in Russia has been not mainly ideological, political, or economic, but biological. Stalin liquidated the most-civilized segment of the Russian population and made of Russia a nation of lower mujiks. Most of the city-bred Russians were killed off, imprisoned, or exiled. She searched the faces in the streets of Moscow: "It was hopeless trying to find one single face which clearly belonged to a born city dweller." How was the pattern of life of these newcomers formed? It has the appearance of an old-fashioned bourgeois world harking back to the period of 1900.

You get the impression that the suspicion and the rudeness which manifest themselves in Russia's foreign dealings are a reflection of the suspicion and rudeness which permeate the lives of the people high and low. Whom does Khrushchev trust? In Russia "even the most commonplace activities assume a sinister air of secrecy." What she holds against the Soviet government is not that it has not been able to provide the citizens of such a rich country with a good life but "the fear which rules men's lives in Russia today." The fear, she thinks, is more degrading than hunger and cold, and is a sign of something rotten within the regime.

Now, Soviet Russia is undoubtedly a going concern with an air of permanence. It does not operate smoothly and efficiently, but it manages to feed, clothe, house, and educate its millions. She was aware of an "all-pervading atmosphere of latent discontent" and of "a clear division between government and people, as if the latter were making a point of dissociating themselves from the former." But my feeling is that if a drastic change takes place in Russia it will come from above. Despite their education, the Russians are still as submissive as Lenin knew them, "so patient, so accustomed to privation."

April 29

Every now and then when I catch myself it is as if I have been quarreling and arguing with someone for days. Yet not a cross word has passed my lips in God knows how long. I am reminded of the time when I worked in the fields, when it sometimes seemed to me that I had been crying for weeks.

April 30

Eight hours on a Pope & Talbot ship at Pier 38. A heavy fog is at this moment (7:20 P.M.) swallowing the city.

I am reading *Wedemeyer Reports*. What startles me most are the quotations from isolationists such as Hoover, Lindbergh, and Professor Spykman about the ultimate results of the Second World War. These people really foresaw our present difficulties and dangers. Clearly, those who narrowed their vision to the interests of America had a better conception of the eventual course of events than those who thought in terms of humanity as a whole, and of the ideals of freedom, justice, democracy, etc. Another way of putting it is that the men who hated Germany least had a better grasp of the future than those who were possessed by an intense loathing for Hitler and his works. Still, one wonders what a corroding effect a sitting-out of the war might have had on this country. A neutral America growing fat on the misery of the rest of the world would have been an abomination to most of us.

May 1

7 P.M. Worked eight hours on the Pope & Talbot *Builder* at Howard. Discharged steel plate. Easy but tense work due to the weight of the plates—seven tons each and they had to be landed in gondolas.

At noon it occurred to me that from Moses to Lenin the intellectuals were convinced that the swinish masses were unfit to enter the promised land. One or more generations had to be sacrificed, and only a new generation reared under the eyes of the schoolmaster-rulers would shape the new world. I am sure that if a Moses or a Lenin had had it in his power to regulate the settling of this continent, he would not have allowed the undesirables from Europe to come over in their millions. Francis Bacon knew beyond doubt that the scum transplanted to the colonies would not work, and would quickly weary.

May 3

As late as the end of the nineteenth century and even up to 1914, there was a sense of stability and permanence in the world. The present became short-lived with the First World War. Thus we have had only fifty years or so to adjust ourselves to a situation of rapid, drastic change. The paradox is that in a time of drastic change the familiar changes from boyhood to manhood, from want to affluence, from work to leisure, from inferiority to equality become difficult and explosive. One of the reasons is that in a time of rapid change there is no room for waiting and patience. We want to leap rather than grow.

Can the human species ever adjust itself to endless, drastic change? Are there instances of living organisms enduring and thriving in an environment without stability and continuity?

I compared the stretched soul to the stretched string of a musical instrument when I said that only a stretched soul makes music. Nietzsche likened the stretched soul to a tensely-strained bow with which one can aim at the furthest goals. The bow is said to have been a musical instrument before it became a weapon.

May 6

Eight hours on the *Samadinda* at Pier 19. An easy and very pleasant day. Head does not work.

May 7

Eight hours on the *Samadinda.* Finished the job.

10 P.M. On the way home I picked up a book in a second-hand bookstore. The title caught my eye: *The Vanished Pomp of Yesterday,* by Lord Frederic Hamilton. Quite often of late there has welled up in me a craving to live in a stable, stagnant, and even decaying society where values and ways have remained unchanged for generations, and no one is going anywhere. Actually the book is about life in the diplomatic world of the last decades of the nineteenth century. It is a chatty book, but on page 135 I found something that startled me: the record of a conversation between the author and a young mujik in a village in northern Russia. What startled me were the similarities between the opinions of a Russian mujik eighty years ago and present-day Communist propaganda. The mujik thought there was no electric light outside Russia since Jablochkov, a Russian, had invented that. Were there roads outside Russia? Could people read and write? Certainly there were no towns as large as Petrograd. Clearly, Communist propaganda has

not been cooked up in the Kremlin but echoes attitudes and beliefs indigenous to a nation made up of lower mujiks. It is probably true that in thinking of Russia one ought not to confuse the victims with their executioners. But it is also true that the two have an awful lot in common.

May 8

Seven hours on the *W. L. Lundgreen* at Pier 41. Last night I hardly slept. I read the Hamilton book until past midnight, and then could not fall asleep. Fortunately today's job was easy. Just now (6:30) I can hardly keep my eyes open.

May 9

Eight hours on the *Gloria Maru* at Pier 39. Started 9 A.M. and finished 6 P.M. If I work tomorrow I shall make a good check. Last week, despite availability, I made only $57 take-home pay.

I slept 9½ hours last night. The long sleep endowed me with patience and good will. I felt at ease all day.

May 11

I just discovered that the last few entries in this diary were dated March instead of May. I apparently forgot the month.

Yesterday I was dispatched to Pier 41 but the ship did not come in. They gave us four hours, sent us home, and ordered us back for today. This morning I found the beautiful French ship *Maryland* tied at the pier. We had an easy, delightful day.

The article on man and nature which I am writing for the *Saturday Evening Post* is coming along fine. Almost every idea in the train of thought has been worked out long ago. What I have to do is dovetail them more or less smoothly. There are a few gaps to be filled. One is the idea that man's creativeness originates in the characteristics which distinguish man from other forms of life. In other words, human creativeness is basically unlike any creative process that may be found in the rest of creation. I also must have a pithy section on the role of magic (words) in human affairs. The title of the article will be "The Unnaturalness of Human Nature." I ought to have it finished and typed before the end of this month.

The fact that I can put together a good article by fitting ideas into a mosaic bothers me a little. It would have done me a world of good to be able to pour forth a stream of writing, to have new ideas gush from my mind onto paper. My sort of writing lacks the quality of catharsis. Yet only writing—any sort of writing—can justify my existence.

May 12

When exploring the differences between civilizations, their attitude toward nature must be given a prominent place. This attitude affects not only religion and the mechanics of everyday life, but the position of the individual and the pattern of freedom and power. The same environment made a nomad of the American Indian and a pioneer of the European immigrant, and in the make-up of the pioneer the Old Testament was a pronounced ingredient.

The downgrading of nature in the Old Testament has been a crucial factor in the emergence of the modern Occident. Jehovah created both nature and man, yet made man in His own image and appointed him His viceroy on earth. The injunction in the first chapter of Genesis is unmistakable: be fruitful and multiply and subdue the earth. If I am not mistaken, the Judaic religion has been the first and only one to separate God and man from nature. In all other religions God and nature are identical. The downgrading of nature in the Old Testament has been at the root of the Occident's aspiration toward freedom and justice, and of its science and technology, which enabled it to master nature on an unprecedented scale.

It is significant that in the Orient, where civilization had its birth, the manmade world of the city did not give its inhabitants a sense of apartness from the predetermined, inexorable, and unalterable nonhuman cosmos. The edict of the temple and of the palace had the implacability of laws of nature. Though the birth of civilization is hardly conceivable without the challenge of new questions, the civilizations of Asia, once established, functioned as if the answers were there before the questions.

Outside the Western tradition the tendency has been to equate power with nature, and bow before tyranny as before a natural cataclysm.

May 13

7 P.M. A light-footed fog is just now drifting over the rim of the amphitheater of the city. It was wet and cold in the morning, hot and sultry in the middle of the day, and now the cool fog.

I can now see my way ahead. When I finish the article on nature and another one on individual freedom I shall have enough manuscript for a small book: a collection of articles, most of them dealing with change in the backward countries. It will be a book on change, but without a comprehensive theory and without an exploration of the various instances of change. The book on change will come later, once the collection of articles is out of the way.

May 20

I twisted the wrist of my right hand six days ago while heaving sacks of nails. Today is the first day's work after a week of oppressive leisure. The bruised hand is almost well.

Today I worked 6½ hours on the *Harunassan Maru* at Pier 26. An easy and pleasant job, and my head is beginning to work.

The book on change will have a chapter on Moses and the Exodus. There is something like a Moses pattern in every instance of drastic change. Moses wanted to turn a tribe of enslaved Hebrews into free men. You would think that all he had to do was gather the slaves and tell them that they were free. But Moses knew better. He knew that the transformation of slaves into free men was more difficult and painful than the transformation of free men into slaves. The change from slavery to freedom requires many other drastic changes. To begin with, a leap from one country to another—a migration. Hence the Exodus. More vital was the endowment of the ex-slave with a new identity and a sense of rebirth. The whole Pentateuch deals with the staging of the drama of rebirth. No playwright and no impresario have ever staged such a grandiose drama. The setting had a live volcano as a backdrop, and the cast included the mighty Jehovah Himself.

What was the denouement? Moses discovered that no migration, no drama, no spectacle, no myth, and no miracles could turn slaves into free men. It cannot be done. So he led the slaves back into the desert, and waited forty years until the slave generation died, and a new generation, desert born and bred, was ready to enter the promised land.

All revolutionary leaders, though they fervently preach change, know that people cannot change. Unlike Moses they have neither a handy desert nor the patience to wait forty years. Hence the purges and the terror to get rid of the grown-up generation.

It is of interest that even in the objective world of science man's mind is not more malleable than in the habit-bound world of everyday life. Max Planck maintained that a new scientific truth does not triumph by convincing its opponents, but because its opponents eventually die, and a new generation grows up that is familiar with it. Here, too, you need forty years in the desert.

May 21

Eight hours on the Pope & Talbot *Voyager* at Pier 38. An easy and pleasant day. Indeed, I was in something like a festive mood all day long. It was partly due to the fact that I had on new working clothes. No one has fully investigated the effect of clothes on man's moods and behavior. Nietzsche said somewhere that a woman who feels well-dressed would not catch a cold even if she were half-naked. Emerson quotes a lady saying that when she is perfectly dressed she has a feeling of inner tranquility which religion is powerless to bestow. I have never been well-dressed; never had on things of perfect fit and excellent material.

The union has taken in five hundred new longshoremen. They have been sifted out of several thousand applicants, and make an excellent impression. It was pleasant to see fresh faces, mostly young, on the dock.

Former migratory worker and longshoreman, Eric Hoffer burst on the scene in 1951 with his irreplaceable tome, *The True Believer*, and assured his place among the most important thinkers of the twentieth century. Nine books later, Hoffer remains a vital figure with his cogent insights to the nature of mass movements and the essence of humankind.

Hoffer in the old San Francisco Public Library

Of his early life, Hoffer has written: "I had no schooling. I was practically blind up to the age of fifteen. When my eyesight came back, I was seized with an enormous hunger for the printed word. I read indiscriminately everything within reach—English and German.

"When my father (a cabinetmaker) died, I realized that I would have to fend for myself. I knew several things: One, that I didn't want to work in a factory; two, that I couldn't stand being dependent on the good graces of a boss; three, that I was going to stay poor; four, that I had to get out of New York. Logic told me that California was the poor man's country."

Through ten years as a migratory worker and as a gold-miner around Nevada City, Hoffer labored hard but continued to read and write during the years of the Great Depression. The Okies and the Arkies were the "new pioneers," and Hoffer was one of them. He had library cards in a dozen towns along the railroad, and when he could afford it, he took a room near a library for concentrated thinking and writing.

In 1943, Hoffer chose the longshoreman's life and settled in California. Eventually, he worked three days each week and spent one day as "research professor" at the University of California in Berkeley. In 1964, he was the subject of twelve half-hour programs on national television. He was awarded the Presidential Medal of Freedom in 1983.

CPSIA information can be obtained at www.ICGtesting.com
Printed in the USA
BVOW061031230512

290890BV00003B/272/P